Springer Series in Cognitive Development

Series Editor
Charles J. Brainerd

Springer Series in Cognitive Development

Series Editor: Charles J. Brainerd

Children's Logical and Mathematical Cognition:
Progress in Cognitive Development Research
Charles J. Brainerd (Ed.)

Verbal Processes in Children:
Progress in Cognitive Development Research
Charles J. Brainerd/Michael Pressley (Eds.)

Adult Cognition:
An Experimental Psychology of Human Aging
Timothy A. Salthouse

Recent Advances in Cognitive-Developmental Theory:
Progress in Cognitive Development Research
Charles J. Brainerd (Ed.)

Learning in Children:
Progress in Cognitive Development Research
Jeffrey Bisanz/Gay L. Bisanz/Robert Kail (Eds.)

Cognitive Strategy Research:
Psychological Foundations
Michael Pressley/Joel R. Levin (Eds.)

Cognitive Strategy Research:
Educational Applications
Michael Pressley/Joel R. Levin (Eds.)

Equilibrium in the Balance:
A Study of Psychological Explanation
Sophie Haroutunian

Crib Speech and Language Play
Stanley A. Kuczaj, II

Stan A. Kuczaj, II

Crib Speech and Language Play

With 154 Figures

Springer-Verlag
New York Berlin Heidelberg Tokyo

Stan A. Kuczaj, II
Department of Psychology
Southern Methodist University
Dallas, Texas 75275
U.S.A.

Series Editor
Charles J. Brainerd
Department of Psychology
University of Alberta
Edmonton, Alberta
Canada T6G 2E9

Library of Congress Cataloging in Publication Data
Kuczaj, Stan A.
  Crib speech and language play.
  (Springer series in cognitive development)
  Bibliography: p.
  Includes index.
  1. Language acquisition. I. Title. II. Series.
  [DNLM: 1. Language development. WS 105.5.C8
  K95c]
  P118.K8 1983   401'.9   83-10402

Typeset by MS Associates, Champaign, Illinois
Printed and bound by R.R. Donnelley and Sons, Harrisonburg, Virginia
Printed in the United States of America.

9 8 7 6 5 4 3 2 1

ISBN 0-387-90860-9 Springer-Verlag New York Berlin Heidelberg Tokyo
ISBN 3-540-90860-9 Springer-Verlag Berlin Heidelberg New York Tokyo

To Brooke. Thanks. . .

Series Preface

For some time now, the study of cognitive development has been far and away the most active discipline within developmental psychology. Although there would be much disagreement as to the exact proportion of papers published in developmental journals that could be considered cognitive, 50% seems like a conservative estimate. Hence, a series of scholarly books devoted to work in cognitive development is especially appropriate at this time.

The *Springer Series in Cognitive Development* contains two basic types of books, namely, edited collections of original chapters by several authors, and original volumes written by one author or a small group of authors. The flagship for the Springer Series is a serial publication of the "advances" type, carrying the subtitle *Progress in Cognitive Development Research*. Each volume in the *Progress* sequence is strongly thematic, in that it is limited to some well-defined domain of cognitive-developmental research (e.g., logical and mathematical development, development of learning). All *Progress* volumes will be edited collections. Editors of such collections, upon consultation with the Series Editor, may elect to have their books published either as contributions to the *Progress* sequence or as separate volumes. All books written by one author or a small group of authors are being published as separate volumes within the series.

A fairly broad definition of cognitive development is being used in the selection of books for this series. The classic topics of concept development, children's thinking and reasoning, the development of learning, language development, and memory development will, of course, be included. So, however, will newer areas such as social-cognitive development, educational applications, formal modeling, and philosophical implications of cognitive-developmental theory. Although it is anticipated that most books in the series will be empirical in orientation, theoretical and philosophical works are also welcome. With books of the latter sort, heterogeneity of theoretical perspective is encouraged, and no attempt will be made to foster some specific theoretical perspective at the expense of others (e.g., Piagetian versus behavioral or behavioral versus information processing).

C. J. Brainerd

Preface

During the course of acquiring their native language, many, perhaps all, children practice their language skills, typically while they are engaging in some form of language play. In her classic work on the crib speech of her son Anthony, Ruth Weir (1962) suggested that this sort of behavior was more likely to occur in crib speech than in social-context speech. Given that this hypothesis is the primary concern of the present volume, I would like to express my gratitude to Ruth Weir for providing the theoretical impetus for this investigation.

In the present book, I report data concerned with the language play (practice) of fourteen children. The children's speech was sampled in two contexts—social-context speech and crib speech. The types and frequency of language play in the two speech sampling contexts were compared in order to ascertain whether the crib speech setting was more likely to yield language play than was the social-context speech setting. The effect of the origin of the model utterance (either produced by the child or by a present other) on subsequent language play was also investigated. Although several general trends emerged from these analyses, there were considerable individual differences and interactions of type of language play, speech-type (crib vs. social-context), and model-type (child vs. other).

I am very grateful to the fourteen children and their parents who participated in the investigation for allowing us to invade their homes. The children were simply delightful, as they are wont to be. The parents were invaluable, both in terms of the interest they took in the project and in terms of collecting the crib speech samples. Many, many thanks to all of you.

I am also grateful to the National Institute of Mental Health (Grant #1 R03 MH 33362-01) and the National Science Foundation (Grant # BNS 7824733) for proᵣiding funds for a longitudinal study of the developmental relations of crib speech and social-context speech. I would like to thank the competent anonymous reviewers of the grant proposals I submitted to each of these agencies. Their written comments resulted in a much improved project.

Literally dozens of students from S.M.U. and the University of Minnesota assisted me with various aspects of this investigation. Although I have already expressed my appreciation to each of them privately, I would like to take this opportunity to thank three of them publicly. I am very grateful to Alice Barton (who began the project as Alice Bean), Rick Boston, and Brooke Harbaugh for their efforts in regard to subject recruitment, data collection, and data analyses. Although other students contributed in each of these areas, these three were invaluable. This book benefited from my discussions with each of them.

I was fortunate to be able to present papers based on parts of the crib speech project at the 1981 biennial meeting of the Society for Research in Child Development and at the 1982 annual meeting of the Midwestern Psychological Association. I thank my colleagues for the informative and insightful comments I received following these presentations.

Special thanks go to Ann Wassel, my secretary par excellence, for her patience and diligence in typing and retyping the manuscript. In addition to deciphering my handwriting, she weathered my bad moods and complaints. Without her, the book would still be in progress.

Steve Whiteman undertook the onerous task of producing each of the Figures that readers will find liberally sprinkled (flooded?) throughout the text. I am deeply appreciative to him for his efforts.

I am also deeply appreciative of the patience and encouragement that Chuck Brainerd exhibited for this project. Chuck was most supportive throughout the entire writing and editing enterprise. The editorial staff of Springer-Verlag took special efforts to prod me along. Once this prodding had achieved the desired effect (a completed manuscript), the production staff at Springer-Verlag took over and did an admirable job with the production end of things. I am grateful to all of them for their help.

Finally, I should like to express my appreciation to those readers who will laboriously sift through the many Tables and Figures that comprise the majority of the book. There is a wealth of data presented throughout the text, and, as always, I have interpreted it in terms of my own biases. Partly to reduce the possibility of my biases affecting the significance of the data, and partly because the data are so abundant, I have elected to provide readers with as much of the data as possible. We all know that science progresses as a result of both new data and new theory. Although this book is more heavily weighted toward new data than new theory (although it does contain both), I hope that it will contribute in both areas. As usual, only time will tell.

Dallas, Texas   Stan A. Kuczaj, II
June, 1983

Contents

Chapter 1	**Introduction**...	**1**
	Language Practice (Play)	3
	Types of Language Practice..................................	3
	Developmental Patterns	5
	Influence of Social Variables on Language Practice...........	8
	Why Do Children Play with Language?	13
	Purpose of this Volume..	18

Chapter 2	**Methodology**	**21**
	Subjects..	21
	Speech Sampling...	22
	Transcription...	23
	Scoring of Speech Samples	23

Chapter 3	**Mean Length of Utterance in Morphemes**...................	**25**
	Group Comparisons...	26
	Analyses of Individual Children's MLU in	
	Various Situations	26
	Discussion	34

Chapter 4   **Linguistic Practice** **37**

                  Group Analyses............................... 37
                  Preliminary Analyses of Individual Patterns 43
                  More Analyses of the Linguistic Practice of
                  Individual Children 49
                  Analyses of Developmental Patterns: Buildups................ 78
                  Analyses of Developmental Patterns: Breakdowns 94
                  Analyses of Developmental Patterns: Completions............ 104
                  Analyses of Developmental Patterns: Exact Reproductions 115
                  Analyses of Developmental Patterns: Substitutions............ 126

Chapter 5   **Discussion, Conclusions, and Speculations** **151**

                  The Relation of Imitation and Repetition 155
                  The Relation of Crib-Speech Practice and
                  Social-Context-Speech Practice 157
                  Parents' Modeling of Linguistic Practice...................... 159
                  Why Do Children Engage in Language Practice?.............. 162
                  Is Crib Speech an Important Context for Language Practice?.. 166

References... 173
Author Index 181
Subject Index 185

1. Introduction

Children learning their first language accomplish a monumental task. During a developmental period in which their cognitive skills are typically regarded as relatively meager or immature (Brainerd, 1978; Flavell, 1963), children acquire with relative ease the complex system that makes possible language comprehension and production. The complexities of the system have resulted in many hypotheses concerning the nature of language, including discussions of its phonological characteristics (e.g., Jakobson, 1968), its syntactic and morphological characteristics (e.g., Chomsky, 1965; Fillmore, 1968), the nature of the lexicon (e.g., Katz, 1972; Leech, 1974; Lyons, 1977), the interaction of discourse needs and intentions with the semantic/syntactic system (e.g., Sadock, 1974; Searle, 1969), and the acquisition of this complex array of knowledge (Maratsos, in press; Wexler & Culicover, 1980). There is considerable disagreement concerning the answers to the key questions in each of the above areas, but one fact is acknowledged by all theorists—between the time of birth and their fifth birthday, children acquire much of their first language, a significant but apparently easy accomplishment on the part of each child.

Language acquisition is a significant achievement for two reasons. First, children acquire a conceptual system that goes far beyond the information provided by the environment. Children hear individual sounds, words, and sentences, but must learn both abstract-form classes such as noun or agent, and rules for manipulating these form classes in some meaningful fashion. These rules and form classes are essential aspects of language and language development, for they allow for language's most important characteristic—its productivity. The productivity of language makes possible the production and comprehension of novel linguistic constructions. Even young children use language in a productive fashion, and so theories of language acquisition must account for the acquisition of both abstract-form classes and the rules that govern the use of the form classes.

The characteristics of the language system should make its acquisition quite difficult, particularly for those with immature cognitive skills. However, children apparently accomplish this feat with relative ease. These features of language development—the difficulty of the task in principle and the relative ease of the task in actuality—have led to considerable debate concerning the nature of first-language acquisition. On the one hand, it has been argued that the phenomenon of language development is best explained in terms of innate knowledge of language (Chomsky, 1959, 1972; McNeill, 1970) or innate processes that underlie language development (Slobin, 1973). On the other hand, it has been argued that children's linguistic environment provides sufficient input to result in the learning of a first language without any unique language-learning capacity (Skinner, 1957). Of course, it seems most likely that the *capacity* for human language is innate, but that the *realization* of this capability depends on a sufficiently rich linguistic environment. The theoretical task thus becomes one of attempting to specify the nature of the innate capability and the nature of the relevant environment variables.

Although I shall not attempt to specify the nature of the innate language-learning capability, the work to be reported in this volume rests on the assumption that language development depends on children's processing of input and the influence of past intake (information children have gleaned from past input) on subsequent processing of input (Kuczaj, 1982a). This view emphasizes the interaction of information processing and organizing predispositions (some innate and others learned) and environmental factors, and at the same time acknowledges the importance of intrinsic motivation in the language-learning processes. Thus, I am attributing great importance to children's experiences and even greater importance to their interpretation of these experiences, the interpretation resting on the internal (mental) context children create in their attempts to assimilate the external context (differences in internal contexts resulting in different children intrepreting the same input in varying ways; see Kuczaj, 1975).

It seems likely that two main types of intake serve to facilitate language development. First, experience with the same item in different contexts and different items in similar contexts leads children to create form classes (Maratsos, 1979; Maratsos, in press; Maratsos & Chalkley, 1980), and to later differentiate form classes (the differentiation occurring because children come to limit the generality of earlier acquisitions; see Kuczaj, 1977, and Kuczaj & Brannick, 1979, for examples). Second, resolvable conflicts between early acquisitions and current intake, which seem crucial for cognitive growth (Piaget, 1963, 1966), are also important for language development (Nelson, 1978, accurately termed such conflicts "codable discrepancies").

Much of the early work on language development focused on children's processing of linguistic information in the absence of any overt behavior on the children's part, the assumption being that most processing of linguistic information occurs at the covert (mental) level rather than the overt behavioral level (e.g., Chomsky, 1959, 1972; McNeill, 1970; Slobin, 1973). More recently, however, there has been a growing concern with the influence of one type of overt behavior on language development—language practice—which typically, but not always, occurs in the context of language play. The tendency to play with language during the course of first-language acquisition seems to be a universal phenomenon (Garvey, 1977; Kuczaj, 1982b), and may thereby have some innate basis, but it seems to be influenced by a number of environmental variables. The most important environmental variables seem to be (a) the presence or absence of others in the speech context, and (b) whether or not the child is attempting to communicate when speaking in the presence of another. Before considering these variables, I shall discuss the nature of language practice and specify the terminology to be used in the remainder of this volume.

Language Practice (Play)

It is difficult to distinguish language play and language practice (Kuczaj, 1982b). For this reason, I shall use the phrase *language practice* to refer to certain types of behaviors that may or may not occur in *the context of* language play. The influence of language practice and language play on language development has been the subject of considerable interest of late (see Kuczaj, 1982b). Rather than review this literature in detail, I will instead focus on the issues more apropos for the topic of this book. Readers interested in more thorough reviews of the literature on the relations among language play and language development are referred to Garvey (1977a, 1977b) and Kuczaj (1982b).

Types of Language Practice

Language practice involves two basic processes: (a) modification and (b) imitation/repetition. Modification involves the alteration of a preceding language behavior, some part of the original utterance being preserved in the modification. Imitation/repetition involves the (sometimes partial) reproduction of a preceding model utterance, which may be provided by the child or by another speaker. In many cases, language play involves both modification and imitation/repetition. Sequences of language play may involve alternations of modifications and imitations/repetitions, as well as modification-imitation/repetition combinations.

Modifications

There are a number of types of modifications that occur in language play (Braine, 1971, 1974; Kulikowski, 1981; Snyder, 1914; Weir, 1962). Following Weir (1962), these types will be referred to as buildups, breakdowns, completions, and substitutions.

Buildups constitute an utterance sequence of two or more parts, each successive part including the words of the previous utterance and additional linguistic units. Examples of buildups are: (a) Block. Yellow block. Look at all the yellow blocks; and (b) Build tower. There build tower now.

Breakdowns are the opposite of buildups. In a breakdown, the first utterance is the longest and most complete. Successive utterances involve the reproduction of parts of the original utterance. Examples of breakdowns are: (a) Clock off. Clock. Off; and (b) This clown fall down. Clown fall down.

A third type of modification sequence is the completion. Completions are not always modifications in the true sense of the term in that the original utterance is not necessarily modified. A completion sequence involves two or more utterances that are separated by a pause (or pauses) but which form a more complex utterance when considered as a combined utterance. Parts of the original utterance may or may not be repeated in the successive utterance(s). Examples of completions are: (a) And put it (pause), up there; and (b) Anthony take the (pause), take the box.

The final type of linguistic practice sequence is the substitution. This consists of a substitution in the second or third utterance of a different word of the same form class in a sentence gramatically parallel to the original utterance. Examples of substitutions are: (a) What color blanket? What color map? What color glass?, and (b) Heather's bad. I'm bad. You bad.

The examples just given are of modifications based on utterances the child produced. These will be referred to as self-model modifications. Other speakers may provide the original utterance for a modification. These will be referred to as other-model modifications.

Imitation/Repetition

One common type of language practice is that in which children repeat all or part of a preceding model utterance. Two categories of such play can be identified: (a) imitation—those instances in which children repeat another person's preceding utterance; and (b) repetition—those instances in which children repeat their own preceding utterance. Both imitations and repetitions may be exact reproductions, reduced reproductions, expanded reproductions, or reduction/expansion combinations. Exact imitations and repetitions consist of complete reproductions of the model, with nothing deleted or added. Reduced imitations and repetitions are those in which part of the model is omitted, but nothing is added. Expanded imitations and repetitions are those in which something is added to the model. In addition, reduction/expansion combinations exist—the imitation or repetition is a reduction of the model utterance but something is added as well. The following examples illustrate each of the above types of imitation and repetition (from Kuczaj, 1982b):

Type of Imitation/Repetition	Mother	Child
1. Exact imitation	Pick those up.	Pick those up.
2. Exact repetition		Cats fall and booms. Cats fall and booms.
3. Reduced imitation	Stop splashing the bubbles all over the bathroom.	Splashing bubbles all the bathroom.
4. Reduced repetition		Craig stand on chair. Stand on chair.

5. Expanded imitation	That's nice.	That's nice song.
6. Expanded repetition		That burns.
		That burns I touch it.
7. Reduced expansion combination/imitation	Please get down.	Get down and stay down.
8. Reduced/expansion combination repetition		Gover's my friend. Grover my friend and Big Bird my friend.

These examples illustrate the difficulty of distinguishing modification and imitation/repetition. Exact imitations and exact reproductions seem to be a unique category. Reduced imitations and reduced repetitions are breakdowns, the former involving a model produced by another speaker and the latter involving a model produced by the child. Expanded imitations and expanded repetitions are buildups, the difference between imitation and repetition again resting on whether another speaker or the child produced the model utterance. At least some reduction/ expansion combinations have the characteristics of substitutions. This overlap between modification and imitation/repetition leads to terminological difficulties. The literature on modifications uses terms such as buildup and breakdown whereas the literature on imitation/repetition employs terms such as reduced imitation and expanded imitation. Partly for the sake of clarity and partly because this is a volume about crib speech, I shall adopt the nomenclature of the literature on children's language-play modifications which Weir (1962) initiated.

Developmental Patterns

Imitation/Repetition

Both imitation and repetition of speech sounds make their first appearance in early infancy (Britton, 1970; Hurlock, 1934; Johnson, 1932; Piaget, 1951, 1963; Valentine, 1942). Children continue to imitate and repeat themselves as they learn words and learn to combine these words to form grammatical utterances (Bohn, 1914; Dore, 1975; Iwamura, 1980; Miller, 1979; Scollon, 1976). Children who are prone to imitate increase this activity until sometime during the second half of the second year of life, after which time imitation begins to decline in frequency (Bowerman, 1973; Keenan, 1977; Piaget, 1962; Valentine, 1930). Similarly, self-repetition begins to decline in frequency at about two years of age (Pickert, 1981). It continues to decline until approximately age 7, after which time it remains at approximately the same level (Rubin, 1979). The rate of decline of imitation and self-repetition most likely depends on both individual differences and the type of imitation or repetition involved (Kuczaj, 1982b; Slobin, 1968).

The initial investigations of children's spontaneous imitations suggested that imitations were not developmentally progressive, at least insofar as grammatical prowess was concerned (Bloom, 1970; Brown & Bellugi, 1964; Ervin, 1964; Menyuk, 1963; Rodd & Braine, 1970). Contrary to these conclusions, Slobin (1968) argued that spontaneous imitations serve many functions and that these functions may vary according to chronological age and developmental period. Slobin noted that parents frequently expand (build up) their children's utterances, as in the following examples (from Kuczaj, 1982b).

Adult	Child
	That Clancy brush.
That is Clancy's brush.	
Do you want to brush him?	

Older Child	Younger Child
	Me push Abe. Ben push Abe.
Ben push me in the wagon.	
You're a big boy.	
	Abe push Ben.
Abe pushed Ben too.	
	Abe boy. Big boy.
Abe is a big boy.	

Slobin (1968) pointed out that parental expansions could be viewed as expanded imitations of children's utterances, and hypothesized that children's imitations of parental expansions might be developmentally significant in two related aspects: (a) In the expansion of a child's utterance, the parent provides a model for a particular type of imitation (the buildup), and (b) this type of imitation may facilitate grammatical development.

There is evidence to support Slobin's hypothesis that parents may provide children with a model of imitation as well as with forms to imitate. Seitz and Stewart (1975) reported a positive correlation between frequency of parental expansions and frequency of imitation in the speech of nine 2-year-olds. Similar results have been reported by Folger and Chapman (1978), who found that the relative frequency with which children imitated their mother's speech was positively correlated with the relative frequency with which mothers imitated their children's speech. Folger and Chapman also found that children were more likely to imitate maternal imitations than other maternal speech acts, this directly supporting Slobin's (1968) hypothesis that parents may provide children with models of imitation. Each of the previously mentioned studies suggests that some parents provide children with a model of imitation as well as with model sentences to imitate. In this sense, children's tendency to imitate may be socially determined (see Kuczaj, 1982b, for a more thorough discussion of this possibility).

Slobin's (1968) second hypothesis, that children's imitation of maternal expansions may facilitate grammatical development, was based on his observation that in expanded imitations children add linguistic forms which were omitted in their original utterances, as revealed in the following example:

Adult	Child
	Dog run.
The dog's running.	
	Dog running.

Slobin noted that two of the children in Brown's (1973) sample tended to imitate less with increasing age and that adults also tended to expand the children's utterances less often with the children's increasing age. Thus, a sensitive period may exist in which expansions are most helpful to the child (i.e., a period in which the child is prone to produce expanded imitations of parental expansions and learn novel forms in the process).

Slobin also observed these age-related changes in children's imitations of parental expansions: (a) reduced imitations (breakdowns) disappeared at an early age, (b) exact imitations disappeared shortly after reduced imitations, and (c) expanded imitations (buildups) persisted for the longest period. Thus, the accuracy of claims that children's imitations are typically reductions of adult models (e.g., Britton, 1970) most likely depends on the developmental period being considered and the nature of the adult model (see also Bowerman, 1973; Kuczaj, 1982b; Snow, 1981).

Type of imitation and type of repetition seem to change in relative frequency during the course of development. The types of changes observed in one child's speech support the notion that imitations and repetitions may facilitate grammatical development (Kuczaj, 1982b). This child eliminated exact and reduced reproductions sooner than expanded reproductions and reduction/expansion combinations. The latter two types of reproductions were consistently longer and/or more complex than the first two types (as assessed by mean length of utterance in morphemes). Moreover, the expanded and combination reproductions were also longer than spontaneous nonreproductive utterances in the same speech samples (see also Bloom, Hood, & Lightbown, 1974, who reported that children who were imitators had higher mean lengths of utterance in morphemes (MLU) in imitations than in spontaneous speech, the opposite being true for children who were nonimitators).

Apparently, both *what* children imitate or repeat (e.g., parental expansions, Slobin, 1968, unfamiliar constituents, Ryan, 1973) and *how* children imitate or repeat models (i.e., the type of imitation or repetition) influence whether or not such processes are viewed as grammatically progressive. In addition to what and how children imitate and/or repeat, *when* they do so also appears to affect the developmental significance of the reproductions. Imitation during the early stages of language development seems most likely to facilitate the acquisition of words (Bloom et al., 1974; Ramer, 1976; Rodgon & Kurdek, 1977; Shipley, Smith, & Gleitman, 1969), whereas imitation and repetition in later development may affect grammatical development (Miller, 1979; Moerk, 1977; Valentine, 1942). This pattern may not hold for all children, however, but only for those children who can be characterized as imitators. The importance of recognizing individual differences in imitation was demonstrated by Bloom et al. (1974).

Bloom et al. (1974) reported a longitudinal investigation of the imitations of six children. They included only spontaneous exact or reduced imitations in their analyses. Of the six children, three were characterized as consistent imitators, two were not (although these two children did imitate from 4% to 31% of the time), and one child was neither a consistent imitator nor a consistent nonimitator. The imitators were most likely to imitate a model immediately, with no intervening utterances between the model and its imitation. The imitators also exhibited a

strong tendency to use certain words only imitatively and others only spontaneously. Moreover, as spontaneous use of a word increased, use of the word in imitations decreased. Therefore, for imitators, imitation of lexical items did appear to be
developmentally progressive. They imitated words that they did not know (and
thus did not use spontaneously), and did not imitate words they used spontaneously. The imitators also seemed to imitate semantic categories and syntactic forms
that they were in the process of acquiring (see also Scollon, 1976). Thus, they did
not imitate those forms that they had firmly acquired, nor those about which they
knew nothing, but rather they imitated only those things which they viewed as
moderately discrepant, that is, things about which they knew something (see also
Kuczaj & Maratsos, 1975; Piaget, 1954). Apparently, if children are imitators,
what they imitate depends on their current state of development. Imitation is an
active process, and imitators appear to find it rewarding because it results in learning. Thus, children are most likely to imitate that about which they have partial
understanding (Guillaume, 1926; Piaget, 1954; Preyer, 1882; Valentine, 1930).

Modifications

The earliest form of modifictions in language play involves sound play (Groos,
1901; Hurlock, 1934; Leopold, 1949; Lewis, 1936). The playful manipulation of
sounds, both in terms of imitation/repetition and modification, appears quite early
in development, and as such appears to be the most primitive type of verbal play
(Garvey, 1977a, 1977b; Weeks, 1979). This type of play continues throughout
early childhood, and from an early age involves rhythm, rhyme, and alliteration
(Piaget, 1951; Stern & Stern, 1928).

As soon as children begin to combine words, the sorts of modifications described
by Weir (1962) occur. Although little longitudinal evidence on this topic is available, and much of the available evidence is fragmentary, the data suggest that playful modifications of syntactic and morphological constructions are most common
from 1;6 (year;month) to 3;6, after which time modifications begin to decline
(Braine, 1971, 1974; Britton, 1970; Craig & Gallagher, 1979; Scollon, 1976; Snyder, 1914; Weeks, 1979; Weir, 1962).

Influence of Social Variables on Language Practice

The importance of situation has been recognized as influential in determining
behavior. As Achenback (1978) has noted,

> The important question is *not* whether a specific setting influences behavior, but
> how one setting influences behavior differently than another, and how consis-
> tent behavior is from one setting to another. (p. 163).

On the other hand, Gleitman (in press) has recently argued that the environment is
relatively unimportant insofar as language acquisition is concerned. Nonetheless,
social context places some obvious limits on language practice and language play.

Self-repetition may occur in the presence or absence of another person, but imitation necessitates another person to provide the model. Modifications may occur in either the presence or absence of another person, as may play with discourse conventions. However, play in social contexts may or may not be the same as play in solitude.

Garvey (1977a, 1977b) suggested the following categories of spontaneous language play: (a) play with noises and sounds, (b) play with aspects of the linguistic system, (c) play with rhymes, speech acts, and so forth, and (d) discourse play. The last two types of play are primarily social. The first two types appear to be primarily nonsocial—not because no one is present when the child engages in the first two types of play, but because such play does not take the present other into account. That is, the play is self-centered rather than social in the true sense of the word. Thus, three types of language play may be discriminated: (a) *solitary play*—individual self-centered play that occurs in solitude; (b) *social-context play*—individual self-centered play that occurs in the presence of others, none of whom are engaged in the play activity; and (c) *social play*—interactive play, or that "statement of engagement in which the successive, non-literal (play) behaviors of one individual are contingent on the nonliteral behaviors of the other person (Garvey, 1976, p. 570)."

Just as play may be characterized as solitary, social-context, or social, children's speech may be classified according to its social context (Kuczaj & Bean, 1982; Piaget, 1929; Vygotsky, 1962). Private speech, social-context speech, and social speech are easily distinguished. For the purposes of this volume, these types of speech may be distinguished in the following manner: (a) *Private speech* is that speech which children produce when alone, (b) *social-context speech* is that speech produced in the presence of others, but which is not produced for any communicative purpose. That is, the speech is not directed toward the present others in any sense. Like private speech, it is speech for the self and so might best be viewed as social-context monologues (Piaget, 1955). (c) *Social speech* is that speech directed toward another with some communicative intent. Such speech may or may not accurately take the other person's perspective into account, but it is nonetheless directed toward the other person.

The primary function of social speech is communication, but communication is not a function of private speech or social-context speech (although practice of communicative skills might occur in the latter two types of speech). The latter types of speech serve a multitude of functions (Fuson, 1979; Kuczaj & Bean, 1982), but I shall focus on the similarities and differences in language practice in the three types of social contexts and the three types of speech contexts. The crucial variables for both social context and speech context are in fact social: the presence or absence of others, and the exclusion or inclusion of the present others in the play or speech activity.

Social-Context Language Practice

In social-context play (that in which another individual is present), the corresponding language practice may be either individual or social. In social play, the language practice will involve an interdependency on the part of the involved individuals (Garvey, 1976). As already mentioned, Garvey (1977a, 1977b) suggested that play with noises and sounds and play with the linguistic system appear to be primarily nonsocial and so occur in private and social-context situations more often than in social ones. Moreover, Garvey suggested that social language play is not produced until relatively late in development. When this type of play occurs, it is most likely to be play with rhymes, word play, fantasy and nonsense, and play with speech acts and discourse conventions (Garvey, 1977a, 1977b). The idea, then, is that although young children may play with language in the presence of others, the play will *not* be part of the social interactions, that is, it will be nonsocial language play (see also Piaget, 1929).

The key word in the previous paragraph is *primarily*. The first types of language play are not always private (or nonsocial in social-context), nor are the latter types always social. For example, Keenan (1974; Keenan & Klein, 1975) reported that her twin sons engaged in social sound play at the age of 1;9, such play occurring in their speech when they were playing together in their bedroom in the early morning hours. In her discussion of this work, Garvey (1977a) suggested that children may need to be very well acquainted with one another in order to engage in this type of social sound play. A number of studies bear on this hypothesis, as well as the notion that social language play is a relatively late development.

Garvey (1977a, 1977b) studied the language play of 48 dyads ranging in age from 2;10 to 5;7. The social language play she observed increased with age, and involved spontaneous rhyming and word play, play with fantasy and nonsense, and play with speech acts and discourse conventions. However, when the children engaged in nonsocial speech (i.e., social-context monologues), they were more likely to produce noise and sound play, word play, and grammatical modifications (although they were less likely to do so than was Wier's son Anthony in his crib speech, Weir, 1962).

Martlew, Connolly, and McCleod (1978) studied the speech of a boy, Jamie, beginning at age 5;6. His speech was observed over a 3-month-period in three conditions: (a) playing alone, (b) playing with one or two friends, and (c) playing with his mother. Jamie's MLU was lowest when alone (3.5), slightly higher when playing with friends (3.7), and highest when playing with his mother (4.3). Imitation and repetition were about as common in solitary and mother-present situations, and least common when playing with the friend, this supporting the notion that children are most likely to imitate those with superior knowledge.

Rubin, Hultsch, and Peters (1971) reported that social-context speech in situations with a familiar other (e.g., a friend or parent) resulted in a higher incidence of verbal repetition and word play (about three to four times more) than was reported in other studies with unfamiliar children or adults (see Fuson, 1979, for a thorough review of the relevant literature; see also Zivin, 1979). Thus, the presence or absence of familiar others appears to be one determining factor of children's language play in private speech.

A related study by Craig and Gallagher (1979) (see also Gallagher & Craig, 1978), investigated the syntactic nonconversational features of monologue speech of nine 2- to 3-year-old children. The data consisted of a 2-hour language sample obtained from each child, the sample containing both child-investigator dialogue and child monologue (typically produced during independent play). The results suggested that the monologues could be best characterized syntactically as "highly structured sequences of revision behavior reflecting a basic metalinguistic performative" (Craig & Gallagher, p. 46). There were many examples of buildups and breakdowns, but relatively few substitutions. Craig and Gallagher concluded that monologues were developmentally significant in that they maintained a constant semantic framework within which syntax could be manipulated. In their words, monologues provide "a stable semantic structure" within which "the child is primarily exploring syntactic variations through revisions of adjacent sentence form" (p. 59). Thus, monologues to Craig and Gallagher appeared to be best characterized as a mechanism permitting analysis on the part of the child. As such, monologues should facilitate language development.

The available literature suggests that language play occurs in both truly social contexts in which the child and others participate and in social contexts in which the child plays alone (or perhaps is ignored by the present others). In both social play and social-context play, children play with the phonological system, the grammatical system, and conversational exchanges (Bohn, 1914; Britton, 1970; Craig & Gallagher, 1979; Garvey, 1977a; Jespersen, 1922; Johnson, 1932; Kleiman, 1974; Shields, 1979; Snyder, 1914).

Crib Speech

Parents with young children in the beginning phases of language learning typically notice that their children engage in monologues when they are alone in their bed prior to going to sleep. This phenomenon appears to be fairly common, but has been subjected to relatively little systematic investigation by developmental psycholinguists. This is surprising in that the available evidence suggests that crib speech plays an important role in the child's acquisition of language.

Weir (1962) presented a detailed analysis of the presleep monologues of her 2-and-one-half-year-old son Anthony, in which she reported that Anthony engaged in various types of grammatical modifications in his presleep speech. These grammatical modifications usually occurred in what Weir referred to as *paragraphs*. Paragraphs are utterance sequences that are set apart by definite pauses and some sort of contextual relationship. Modifications such as buildups, breakdowns, completions, and substitutions are found within paragraphs. As a result of these observations, Weir suggested that Anthony's presleep monologues were important in that they allowed Anthony to practice his language skills. From Weir's discussion, it appears that Anthony practiced linguistic structures in these presleep monologues that he did not employ in his spontaneous social-context speech. However, Weir failed to obtain detailed information about Anthony's spontaneous social speech (though notes were apparently kept about Anthony's social-context speech), and so no direct comparison between structures produced in presleep monologues and those produced in social speech is possible.

Moreover, it is not clear that the findings based on Anthony can be generalized to any extent. At the time of the study, he was troubled by sibling rivalry (a younger brother had recently been born) and some of his language skills were regressing, perhaps as a result of his discontent. In addition, the Weir household evidently had an international flavor, so that Anthony was constantly exposed to a number of different English accents and dialects. Anthony also "spent a good deal of time by himself, in his own room, having been taught that this was his proper place" (Weir, 1962, p. 27). This behavior differs from that of the children whose spontaneous speech I have studied previously (Kuczaj, 1976a, 1977; Kuczaj & Maratsos, 1975; Maratsos, Kuczaj, Fox, & Chalkley, 1979).

In spite of these possible shortcomings, Weir's work gains support from other investigations of crib speech. Presleep monologues have been reported as long as 60 years ago (Jespersen, 1922). Jespersen (1922) reported that Danish children engaged in presleep monologues in which they practiced sentences with frequent substitutions of words. This finding supports Weir's observations of Anthony.

A recent study by Black (1979) compared the crib speech and social-context speech of a boy from 2;2 to 2;4. This child engaged in more repetitions of certain morphemes in crib speech than in social-context speech. Language play and spontaneous repairs were more frequent in crib speech than in social-context speech. These findings suggested to Black the possibility that crib speech facilitates morphological development in that it allows the child to choose the topics and contexts of overt speech. This aspect of crib speech corresponds to many of the features of play that seem to make play such an enjoyable enterprise for the young child (and older child and adult, for that matter).

Similar findings and conclusions have been reported by Britton (1970), who reported on the crib speech of a girl at the age of 2;8. This girl's crib speech contained a number of substitutions, such as

but I don't be sick like this
but I don't be sick in bed
but I don't be sick on the bed

Given these results, Britton concluded that crib speech (and language play) was characterized by a freedom (due to lack of communicative intent) on the child's part to use free association to call to mind the next words in a sequence, the associations being either phonological, structural, or semantic. He also suggested that crib speech was the speech in which children first used language not tied to the here and now. Piaget (1951, p. 222) also reported that the first evidence of a child's use of a word to recall an absent something came in crib speech at age 1;7.

Another recent study of crib speech was conducted by Pickert (1981). She compared the crib speech of her own child, Mary Alice, between the ages of 28 months and 52 months, to that of Anthony Weir during the age range 28–30 months. She determined the extent to which their crib speech could be considered to be dialogue, the general trends of development, and the possible influence of crib speech on social development. She found that dialogue constituted a considerable portion of crib speech and that the constitution of these dialogues became more sophisticated over time as the child's language and social competence developed.

The remaining research on crib speech is concerned with the dual crib speech of twin boys at the age of 2;9 (Keenan, 1974; Keenan & Klein, 1975). Imitations, repetitions, and some completions were observed in the data. Keenan (1974) suggested that repetition functioned as an attention-getting device and that imitations functioned primarily as an acknowledgment of the other's utterance. Keenan noted that the direction of the "dialogue" seemed to be influenced more by the phonological properties of the utterances than by semantic considerations. "Real" words were rarely used in sound play sequences. It seems likely that the early language play of twins may be quite unique (Garvey, 1977a, 1977b). At the very least, the crib speech of twins differs from that of other children in that another person is present.

Why Do Children Play with Language?

Typically, play is defined as those activities that are produced spontaneously and for which extrinsic rewards are either nonexistent or secondary (Lewis, 1936; Kuczaj, 1982b; Patrick, 1914; Vinacke, 1974). Children obviously enjoy play, and even the casual observer might be led to conclude that, to the child, play is its own reward. However, what is it about play that the child finds so intrinsically satisfying?

The intrinsic reward for play appears to be the control that the child possesses in play situations (Britton, 1970; Lewis, 1936). While playing, the child is in control of the situation, creating processes and results more or less at will. The child's control of the play situation is greatest for individual play and social-context play (Reynolds, 1976), and is also evident in social play, although in social play each child's freedom and control is at least somewhat constrained by virtue of interacting with the present others (Garvey, 1974, 1976).

The presence of control over the situation and its outcomes seems to be one of the primary reasons why children play. What is it, though, that determines the content of children's play (that is, what they play with)? Children seem most likely to play with that which they are in the process of acquiring (Britton, 1970; Piaget, 1962, 1966; Vygotsky, 1966). The basic assumption of this view is that by virtue of the control children enjoy in play situations, they become able to consolidate acquisitions that they are able to manipulate in the play situation (Piaget, 1962, referred to this process as functional or reproductory assimilation). The impact of playful manipulation of behaviors on the development of these behaviors is thought to occur not only because of the degree of control children have in play situations, but also because the play situation is one in which children may freely simulate behavior. As such, children may create situations in which they can engage in activities in which the normal consequences of such activities are absent (Piaget, 1966; Reynolds, 1976). Thus, children can experiment without worrying about normal consequences, but at the same time learn from the experiences. Play, then, permits experimentation and feedback in the absence of real-world consequences.

The implication of all this is that play is developmentally progressive, in that children seem most likely to play with those behaviors which they are in the process of acquiring. If one assumes that practice facilitates the acquisition of skills, it becomes an important form of learning (Cazden, 1976; Elkonin, 1971). Along these lines, many theorists have suggested that language play is developmentally progressive, assisting the child in the acquisition of various aspects of the linguistic system (Cazden, 1976; Chao, 1951; Davison, 1974; deLaguna, 1927; Elkonin, 1971; Jespersen, 1922; Johnson, 1932; Stern & Stern, 1928). The available data support the notion that language play is developmentally progressive, although children certainly play with aspects of language after these aspects have been stably acquired (Kuczaj, 1982b). Language play during the course of acquisition presumably has mastery as its primary function, whereas language play after mastery has enjoyment as its primary function. Thus, during the course of acquisition of a given aspect of linguistic knowledge, language play serves two functions: Early in the acquisition, language play serves a practice function and thereby facilitates the acquisition of the form; later, after mastery (or perhaps after some degree of mastery), play with the form is truly playful.

Imitation/Repetition

Piaget described the basic relation between practice and knowledge acquisition in the following manner in his consideration of imitation:

> It is true that . . . it is only models which have some analogy with the children's schemas which give rise to imitation. Those which are too remote from the child's experience leave him indifferent, as for instance unfamiliar movements . . . . But sounds and movements which are new to the child, and yet comparable to those he has already made, give rise to an immediate effort at reproduction. The interest thus appears to come from a kind of conflict between the partial difference which attracts his attention the more because it is an obstacle to immediate reproduction. It is therefore this two-fold character of resemblance and opposition which seems to be the incentive for imitation. (Piaget, 1962, pp. 50–51).

There is support in the language-development literature for the emphasis that Piaget (1974) placed on the importance of moderately discrepant events (those somewhat familiar and somewhat novel). Ryan (1973) hypothesized that children tend to imitate unfamilar utterances more often than familiar ones. She suggested that even though children might not reproduce complex adult forms exactly, they could learn from such imitative attempts if they noticed the mismatch between the adult utterance and their own imitative attempts. Ryan also cited an unpublished case study by Leiven in which the child's imitations were developmentally progressive. The child's imitations contained a greater number of different lexical items and fewer routine phrases than did her spontaneous speech. The child also rarely imitated words that she used spontaneously. The importance of imitation for this child was illustrated by the fact that in one spontaneous speech sample, 55% of the child's two-word utterances were preceded by the mother's using both words, and 87% of the two-word utterances were preceded by the mother's using at least one of the two words. Therefore, Ryan concluded that imitation can be developmentally progressive for both lexical items and grammatical forms (see also Bloom et al., 1974).

Other evidence indicates that children are more likely to imitate those with superior knowledge (e.g., parents) than those with less or identical knowledge (e.g., peers; Heibert & Cherry, 1978; Martlew et al., 1978). Imitation may be developmentally progressive by virtue of its selectivity. Children seem most likely to imitate those from whom they may learn something. This possibility may also prove true for repetitions. Children may be most likely to repeat themselves when they are trying to consolidate their knowledge of some aspect of the language system. Of course, there are functions other than the facilitation of learning that imitation or repetition may serve, for example, social maintenance or emphasis. I am purposely emphasizing the developmental facilitation function in this volume.

Although imitation may not be a necessary component of the language-development process (given the individual differences that have been found), it does appear to be important for those children who are imitators. One way in which imitation may facilitate grammatical development is that reproduction permits the continuation of information processing to occur (Bloom et al., 1974; Clark, 1974, 1975, 1977, 1982). Such processing may nonetheless by incomplete. Clark (1977, 1982) has suggested that imitation includes mechanical elements, and that at least some novel forms enter the child's repertoire as a result of this mechanical aspect of imitation. She has also suggested that imitation may be a form of overt rehearsal that children engage in before they can rehearse silently (Clark, 1975), and that they have a "plagiarism" strategy, such that they pad an utterance with portions of the preceding adult model (see also Snow, 1981). Clark also hypothesized that children may engage in holistic processing of adult utterances (see also Brown & Bellugi, 1964), such that they can store the utterances in the form in which they perceive them, and later reproduce these underanalyzed forms. This hypothesis places considerable importance on delayed (or deferred) imitation (see Piaget, 1963; Snow, 1981). However, the status of deferred imitation qua imitation is unclear (e.g., see Leonard & Kaplan, 1976; Kuczaj, 1983). Nonetheless, young children seem quite likely to begin producing multiword utterances by using what have been called rote or routine processes (Clark, 1974, 1977, 1978, 1982; MacWhinney, 1978, 1982). Rote has been defined as follows:

> The central characteristic of rote processing is the absence of any form of analysis. Forms that are learned by rote and applied by rote are never broken up into their component pieces or decomposed in any way. (MacWhinney, 1978, p. 1)

MacWhinney (1975, 1976) demonstrated that young children may initially use rote to correctly produce forms like *horses* and irregular forms like *went* (see also Cazden, 1968; Kuczaj, 1977). Hakuta (1974) also discussed the possibility of learning syntactic structures in some underanalyzed fashion. In particular, he discussed the notion that children may learn language on the level of surface structure (see also Kuczaj, 1982a). He emphasized the "learning through rote memorization of segments of speech without knowledge of the internal structure of those speech segments" (p. 287). Following Brown (1968, 1973), Hakuta called memorized wholes (e.g., *what's that*?) "prefabricated routines." More interesting, however, were what Hakuta termed "prefabricated patterns," which consist of constant segments of sentences which operate in conjunction with variable units, and as such are substitutions in the nomenclature of this volume. For example, the child might use *where is* as the constant portion and insert different but appropriate noun phrases in the appropriate sentential slot depending on the context. Although Hakuta discussed these phenomena in the context of second-language acquisition, similar phenomena have subsequently been observed in the speech of children learning their first language (Blank, Gessner, & Esposito, 1979; Ferrier, 1978).

It seems, then, that children may use imitation as a means of producing grammatical forms that they have not yet sufficiently analyzed into their component parts (Clark, 1977, 1982; Ferguson, 1976; Kuczaj, 1982a). Eventually, routines and other unanalyzed and underanalyzed segments come to be analyzed by the child and so become more productive and less routine-like. This occurs because syntactic development depends on the comparison and relation of known forms, rules, and structures (including rote forms and routines) with new input (Kuczaj, 1982a; Maratsos, in press; Maratsos & Chalkely, 1980).

Thus, imitation and repetition may be important aspects of the language-learning process. Scollon (1976) suggested that imitation and repetition are two phases of one language-learning process. Imitation provides the means for children to practice contrasts that are not yet within their productive system in that the model utterance produced by another may exceed children's linguistic competence. Repetition provides the means for elaborating the system from within and testing it against the model system in that children provide the model and its reproductions. If this is true, then imitation should decrease with the development of a particular linguistic form, while repetition of the linguistic form should increase with development (at least until the form is stably acquired).

Modifications

Braine (1971) suggested that one type of modification, the "replacement sequence," is an important aspect of grammatical development. He used the term replacement sequence rather than the terms suggested by Weir (1962) because he viewed Weir's notion of sequence as too broad in that thematically related sequences were not excluded from Weir's analysis. Replacement sequences are those that are structurally related to one another, usually via expansion (and so are "buildups" in Weir's terminology). However, some replacement sequences also involve substitutions and completions. According to Braine, replacement sequences may help the child to achieve final mastery of a linguistic rule. If so, then the use of such practice patterns in social-context speech or crib speech might be expected to facilitate children's acquisition of their mother tongue, as argued previously by Snyder (1914) and Weir (1962).

Support for Braine's suggestions comes from recent investigations of children's "repairs," utterance sequences in which children spontaneously modify and typically improve the quality of their own utterances.[1] Children begin to engage in repairs soom after they have begun to produce utterances in their native language (Cherry, 1978; Gallagher, 1977; Reilly, 1981; Rogers, 1978). Repairs occur in both intrasentential and intersentential contexts, and invariably involve some sort of modification. Clark and Andersen (1979) reported that 2-year-old children frequently engaged in phonological repairs (e.g., *they don't wear clothes to [bi] −to bed!*), morphological repairs (e.g., *you know what they ate of, eat out of*), lexical repairs (e.g., *what−who's that?*), and syntactic repairs (e.g., *the kitty cat is−de− de spider's kissing the kitty cat's back*). Similar findings have been reported by Leopold (1949, Vol. 4), McTear (1981), and Zakharova (1973). Clark and Andersen (1979) distinguished repairs to the linguistic system from repairs for the listener. The latter are apparently motivated by communicative needs, while the former seem to be motivated by the acquisition task, in that repairs to the linguistic system seem to concern those aspects of the linguistic system that children are in the process of acquiring, such that repairs seem intimately connected to a growing awareness and mastery of the system. This fits well with the notions of "moderate" and "codable" discrepancy that were discussed earlier.

Along these same lines, Reilly (1981) emphasized children's use of repairs as a language-learning device. She suggested that repairs involve a two-step coding process: (a) The child first focuses on encoding the most functionally salient form. (b) The child next focuses on refining or expanding some specific linguistic aspect of the initial utterance. Reilly argued that the two-step coding process of repairs is used by children to practice those aspects of language that they are in the process of acquiring, and that in many cases children can only produce a complex structure immediately after producing an elliptical counterpart. The evidence for Reilly's claims comes from data she collected on 25 children ranging in age from 1;6 to 7;0. The supporting data are of two types. First, there were second turns (repairs) that exceeded the child's normal linguistic first-turn competence, suggesting that the children needed two turns to produce the more complex structure. Second, there were instances in which a particular structure was only produced by a child in a second turn at one age, but in a first turn at a later age, this also suggesting that the child used the second turns to facilitate the use and acquisition of new structures. The second turns that Reilly discussed included buildups (e.g., *all furniture, go find all furniture*) and substitutions (*go find all furniture, look all furniture*) as well as other types of repairs.

---

[1] Repairs do not always lead to more correct forms. Occasionally a repair will replace a correct item with an incorrect one. For example, one of the children studied by McTear (1981) produced the following correction—*and she ate, she eated daddy bear porridge.* This is important in that just as children's errors provide evidence of their linguistic system, children's corrections provide evidence of what the child *views* as errors (Iwamura, 1980; Karmiloff-Smith, 1979; McTear, 1981; Savic, 1980).

Reilly posited that children's first utterances in repair (modification) sequences reflect their "automatic" competence at that particular level of development. By holding the structure of the first utterance constant, children then become able to concentrate on refining or expanding some aspect of the structure. Thus,

> Learning a construction becomes a continuous process where the child builds on what he can already produce, by being free to experiment with new aspects of a structure on the second turn. (Reilly, 1981, p. 13)

This type of behavior implies that children have access to more forms than they can produce on first turns (see also Kuczaj & Maratsos, 1975), given that they correct or refine initial forms. Reilly suggested that this access is to forms that are just beyond children's first-turn capability (i.e., in the process of learning; see also Braine, 1971).

Reilly also noted that children make use of the utterances produced by others to help build more complex utterances (see also, Greenfield & Smith, 1976; Keenan, Schieffelin, & Platt, 1976; Bloom, Rocissano, & Hood, 1976; Scollon, 1979). She suggested that there are considerable functional (i.e., developmental) similarities between children's repairs and their use of others' utterances to help build more complex utterances. This notion has also been advanced in the literature on imitation, and will be one of the concerns of this volume.

Purpose of this Volume

The preceding discussion has emphasized the possibility (more likely, the certainty) that children's practice and play with language facilitates language development. Although all play is not practice and all practice is not play, during the early language-learning years much practice of language occurs in a playful context. As such, language practice and language play are intimately related. Perhaps the relation between language practice (play) and language acquisition is as intimate.

The types of linguistic practice that were discussed earlier seem likely to be particularly good language-learning devices for the young language-learning child to employ. In this type of practice, children either produce the model or initial utterance or have the model utterance provided by another, and then repeat or modify the model utterance. A reasonable working hypothesis suggests itself. If children are able to use language practice to establish and/or resolve moderately discrepant information, then the period of frequent playful modifications and reproductions (imitation and repetition) (1;6 to 3;6) has to do with the amount and nature of linguistic information that children acquire, organize, and consolidate during this 2-year period. The decline of this type of play after 3;6 has to do with the mastery of language that children have achieved by this age.

The preceding discussion has illustrated the concern in the literature with two distinct but related phenomenon: (a) the relation of language practice and language development, and (b) the influence of social setting on children's behavior. In the present volume, I shall report the results of an investigation in which the relation of language practice and social setting was examined. Five types of language practice and two main types of social setting will be considered. The five types of language practice are: (a) exact repetitions and imitations, (b) buildups, (c) breakdowns, (d) completions, and (e) substitutions. The two types of social setting are: (a) crib speech and (b) social-context speech. Within the social-context–speech setting, social speech and asocial speech will be distinguished for certain analyses. By comparing practice-type and social setting, I hoped to ascertain the significance of social setting for language practice.

In addition to this primary concern, the research to be reported herein has the following secondary concerns: (a) What is the extent of individual differences in the frequency of types of linguistic practice? (b) What effect does the origin of the model have on various types of language practice? There are likely to be important processing differences in the reproduction and/or modification of a preceding utterance depending upon whether the model was produced by one's self or by another. In the former case, the model is by definition within one's productive competence. In the latter case, particularly for the young language-learning child, the model may be beyond the listener's productive competence. The processing of model utterances within one's productive competence should differ from that of model utterances beyond one's productive competence. Of particular concern in the present volume will be the frequency of each type of language practice when the original utterance was produced by the child or by an adult. (c) What is the relation of imitation and repetition? Although imitation appears to be affected by individual differences, there is little information in the literature concerning the susceptibility of repetition to individual differences. Children who are imitators may also be self-repeaters, but as noted above, there may be differences depending on the origin of the model utterance (self vs. other). (d) Do parents influence their children's language practice? More specifically, do parents provide models for types of language practice? (e) What is the relationship of MLU in crib speech to the MLU of social-context speech? If crib speech serves as a trying ground for new acquisitions, one might expect MLU in crib speech to consistently exceed that of social-context speech. (f) What is the relationship of MLU and frequency of use of various types of language practice? If language practice does facilitate language development, then this facilitation may be reflected in a relation between MLU and frequency of language practice.

2. Methodology

In this chapter, the methodological characteristics of the investigation will be presented. This brief description is intended to acquaint the reader with the basic methodological aspects of the present study. More detailed descriptions of scoring decisions and analyses will be provided where appropriate in later chapters.

Subjects

Fourteen first-born children (seven males and seven females) participated in the present investigation. Children were selected for participation according to the following criteria: (a) linguistic prowess (the minimum necessary competence being the use of single word utterances); (b) the use of presleep speech monologues (crib speech); (c) clarity of speech (to facilitate the accuracy of transcribing and interpreting the recorded speech samples); and (d) willingness of the parents to participate in the investigation. Thirty-eight sets of children and parents were interviewed after the parents had indicated a willingness to participate. For one or another reason, 24 children were not selected for participation, the remaining 14 children forming the sample from which the data base of the present investigation was obtained.

The primary bases for subject selection were clarity of speech and incidence of crib speech. Once children were selected for participation, their speech was sampled until they ceased to produce crib speech. The children ranged in age from 15 to 24 months at the beginning of their participation. The length of time each child participated ranged from 6 to 27 weeks, each child's participation ceasing when the child stopped producing crib speech. The age and sex of the child and the number of social- and crib-speech samples obtained from each child are given in Table 2-1.

Table 2-1. Characteristics of Each of the 14 Subjects

S	Sex	Age Range (in months)	Number of Social-Context Speech Samples	Number of Crib-Speech Samples
A	M	15–17	11	10
B	M	15–17	7	7
C	M	15–22	27	27
D	F	16–19	11	9
E	M	16–20	12	12
F	F	17–20	10	10
G	F	17–21	13	13
H	F	17–22	21	21
I	F	18–19	6	6
J	F	19–23	14	14
K	M	19–25	24	24
L	M	20–23	11	11
M	M	24–26	9	9
N	F	25–30	19	19

Speech Sampling

In order to obtain as large a speech corpus as possible, weekly audio recordings of 45 to 60 minutes in length were made of both social-context speech and crib speech, except when illness or family vacations prevented speech sampling. The speech sampling conditions follow.

Social-Context Speech

Each social-context-speech sample was recorded in an uninterrupted 45–60 minute period with a Superscope C-205 cassette recorder and a Sony ECM 280 microphone. The recording took place in the child's home with an investigator and at least one parent present. The investigator visited the child's home a minimum of two times prior to the first recording session in order to allow the child to become familiar with the investigator. The investigator brought the child several toys with which to play during the rapport-establishing visits. Other toys were periodically given to the child by the investigator in order to maintain the child's interest. The same investigator was present during the recording of all spontaneous social-context-speech samples for a given child. During each recording session, the investigator made contextual notes in order to facilitate accurate transcription of the recording.

Crib Speech

The crib-speech samples were rarely recorded in uninterrupted 45–60 minute samples because the amount of time spent producing this type of speech varied from child to child and from night to night for the same child. The crib-speech samples obtained each week for a given child most often consisted of crib speech produced on two or more consecutive nights.

By definition, no one other than the child could be present during the taping of the crib-speech samples. As a result, no contextual notes were available for the transcription and interpretation of these audio recordings. Moreover, neither the parents nor the investigator were allowed to enter the child's room to turn on the tape recorder. Such entrances by others were viewed as likely to disrupt the child's crib speech. In order to avoid this problem, a Superscope C-205 cassette recorder with a Sony ECM 280 microphone attached to a 40-foot extension cord was used to record crib speech. The microphone was placed within 3 feet of the child's bed, the 40-foot extension cord allowing the placement of the recording unit in the hall outside the child's room. This enabled the parents to operate the recorder without disturbing the child. For the recording of the crib speech, then, the parents were responsible for turning on the recorder when the child was engaging in crib speech and turning off the recorder when the child had fallen asleep or stopped vocalizing.

Transcription

All recorded speech samples were transcribed by the investigator who was present during the recording of the spontaneous social-context-speech samples. These transcriptions were done within 10 days of the recording session. In order to assess the reliability of the transcriptions, another investigator transcribed 100 consecutive child utterances (and all of the intervening parental and investigator utterances in the social-context-speech samples) from each tape. These reliability checks were made for each tape obtained for each child. The agreement for the two transcriptions for each tape ranged from 90.3% to 100%.

Scoring of Speech Samples

Before discussing the scoring of the speech samples, social-context speech and crib speech will be defined. For the purposes of this investigation, social-context speech and crib speech are defined as follows: (a) *social-context-speech* is defined here as speech produced in the presence of others. This definition does not necessitate an attempt by the child to communicate with the present person(s). The crucial variable is the presence or absence of people when the child is talking, not whether the child is speaking to the present person(s). This definition was adopted in order to allow comparisons of the child's linguistic practice in social speech contexts with his linguistic practice in crib speech. Linguistic play, in the context of social-context speech, need not be directed toward the present person(s), and so defining social-context speech as that directed toward present others would by definition exclude much linguistic practice from the category of social-context speech, an undesirable effect here. In addition, my previous research involving the sampling of children's spontaneous speech (Kuczaj, 1976, 1977) leads me to believe that children frequently engage in monologues in the presence of others, as does the work of Garvey (1977a, 1977b; see also, Piaget, 1955). These monologues are not directed toward the present person(s) and may or may not consist of much linguistic play, depending on what the child is doing at the time (talking to a doll, pretending to be the captain of a ship issuing orders to his subordinates, repeating a linguistic construction or form, etc.). Although this definition of social-context speech includes both speech directed to others (social speech) and speech produced with no (apparent) communicative intent (asocial speech), many of the analyses to be reported later compare these two types of social-context speech. (b) *Crib speech* is defined here as the speech which children produce when alone in their bedroom prior to going to sleep.

The social-context-speech samples and the crib-speech samples were scored for the following: (a) *mean length of utterance in morphemes (MLU),* a rough estimator of productive grammatical capability (Brown, 1973). Comparing the MLUs of each child's social-context speech and crib speech was intended to serve as a heuristic for determining structural differences that might exist between social-context speech and crib speech. (b) *Linguistic practice:* Both the social-context-speech samples and the crib-speech samples were analyzed for evidence of linguistic practice, defined here as utterance sequences involving buildups, breakdowns, completions, substitutions, or exact reproductions.

3. Mean Length of Utterance in Morphemes

This chapter is concerned with the children's means length of utterance in morphemes (MLU) for each of the speech samples. MLU is a gross indicator of syntactic complexity, and as such is also a gross indicator of syntactic development. In the present study, MLU will be used to make gross comparisons of the developmental differences between social-context speech and crib speech, as well as to provide a rough idea of each child's stage of grammatical development (see Brown, 1973, for relevant comparison data and a discussion of the use of MLU as an indicator of grammatical development).

MLU was calculated following the procedures outlined in Brown (1973), with minor deviations from Brown's procedure. The exact procedure used for calculating MLUs was as follows: (a) Start with the first page of the transcription unless that page involves a recitation of some sort. In this latter case, start with the first recitation-free stretch. Count the first 100 child utterances that satisfy the following rules to calculate the MLU for that sample. (b) Use only fully transcribed utterances. Do not use utterances which contain unintelligible portions. (c) Include all exact-utterance repetitions. Stuttering and false starts count as repeated efforts at a single word or phrase. Count the word or phrase once in the most complete form produced in repeated effort. However, in cases where a complete word or phrase is repeated, count each occurrence. (d) Do not count fillers such as *mm* or *oh,* but do count all nonfiller words (e.g., *no, yeah, hi*). (e) All compound words (two or more free morphemes; e.g., *birthday*), proper names, and ritualized reduplications count as single words. Examples include *grandpa, choo-choo, quack-quack, night-night,* and *see-saw.* This decision is justified by the lack of evidence that the constituent morphemes function as constituent morphemes (i.e., young children do not seem to be actually combining the morphemes to produce the compound word; rather they seem to use the terms as underanalyzed wholes). (f) Count as one morpheme all diminutives (e.g., *doggie*). These terms also appear to be learned as underanalyzed wholes by the young child. (g) Count as separate morphemes all auxiliaries (e.g., *is, have*) and all catentatives (e.g., *gonna, wanna, hafta*). (h) Count as separate morphemes all inflections (e.g., possessive [s], plural [s], third person singular [s], regular past [ed], progressive [ing]).

Group Comparisons

The overall MLU for crib speech was obtained by averaging the MLUs for each crib-speech sample for each child. This same procedure was used to determine the overall MLU for the children's social-context speech. The results were as follows: (a) overall crib-speech MLU—2.3; (b) overall social-context-speech MLU—2.4. These numbers do not support the notion that crib speech is developmentally progressive in comparison to social-context speech, in that crib speech is not more complex (i.e., it does not contain more morphemes per utterance) than social-context speech. However, this group comparison ignores a number of important factors, including individual differences and developmental patterns.

Analyses of Individual Children's MLU
in Various Situations

In this section, each child's crib-speech MLU and social-context-speech MLU will be compared. These comparisons for individual children will demonstrate both the extent of developmental consistency across children and the extent of individual differences.

Child A

There was no straightforward relationship between crib-speech MLU and social-context-speech MLU (Figure 3-1). There were nonetheless several interesting patterns. First, there was a substantial decline in social-context-speech MLU followed by a substantial increase and then another substantial decrease. Second, dramatic increases and decreases in MLU were also apparent for crib speech, although the changes were not as great for crib-speech as for social-context-speech MLU. Third, there was an inverse relation for some of the peaks and valleys for crib-speech MLU and social-context-speech MLU. Some of the peaks for social-context-speech MLU occurred when a dip in crib speech MLU occurred, and vice versa.

Child B

The MLUs of Child B provide an interesting comparison with those of Child A in that both children were male and were studied during the same age range (15–17 months old) (Figure 3-2). As seen by comparing Figures 3-1 and 3-2, the MLUs of Child B reflect different developmental patterns than those of Child A. First, crib-

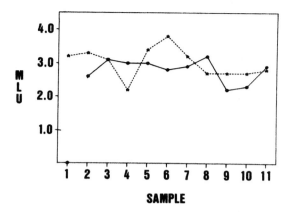

Figure 3-1. Crib-speech and social-context-speech MLUs for Child A. Solid line indicates crib-speech MLU. Dashed line indicates social-context-speech MLU.

speech MLU was usually higher than social-context-speech MLU. Second, rate of development seemed to be more rapid for Child B than for Child A, as well as slightly less erratic. However, there were also similarities in the MLU comparisons of the two children. There were developmental dips and peaks in both crib-speech MLU and social-context-speech MLU. However, they appeared to be more dramatic for crib speech than for social-context speech for Child B. The inverse relation for peaks and valleys for social-context speech MLU and crib speech MLU also occurred for Child B, particularly in the later samples.

Child C

Again, there was no consistent developmental relation between the two types of MLUs (Figure 3-3). Social-context-speech MLU was typically higher than that of

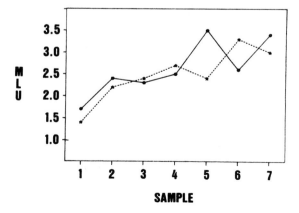

Figure 3-2. Crib-speech and social-context-speech MLUs for Child B. Solid line indicates crib-speech MLU. Dashed line indicates social-context-speech MLU.

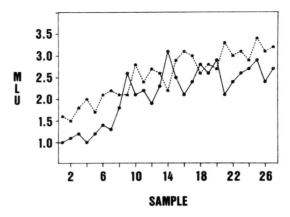

SAMPLE

Figure 3-3. Crib-speech and social-context-speech MLUs for Child C. Solid line indicates crib-speech MLU. Dashed line indicates social-context-speech MLU.

crib speech, but not always. There were many developmental peaks and dips for both social-context-speech MLU and crib-speech MLU. Once again, there was an inverse relation between many of the peaks and valleys for crib-speech MLU and social-context-speech MLU.

Child D

Crib-speech MLU tended to be higher than social-context-speech MLU for Child D (Figure 3-4). The figure also reveals peaks and valleys for both crib-speech MLU and social-context-speech MLU, as well as an inverse relation between some of the peaks and valleys for crib speech and social-context speech. MLU variability was greater for crib speech than for social-context speech.

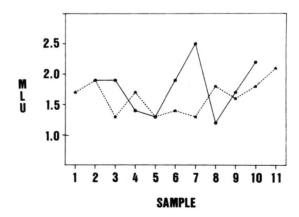

SAMPLE

Figure 3-4. Crib-speech and social-context-speech MLUs for Child D. Solid line indicates crib-speech MLU. Dashed line indicates social-context-speech MLU.

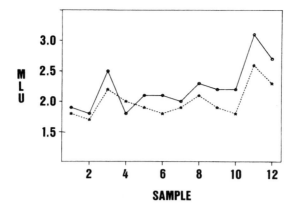

Figure 3-5. Crib-speech and social-context-speech MLUs for Child E. Solid line indicates crib-speech MLU. Dashed line indicates social-context-speech MLU.

Child E

Crib-speech MLU tended to be higher than social-context-speech MLU (Figure 3-5). There were also peaks and valleys in both crib-speech and social-context-speech MLU. However, rather than an inverse relation, the peaks and valleys for crib speech and social-context speech tended to coincide with one another.

Child F

The MLUs for Child F were not consistently higher in crib speech or social-context speech (Figure 3-6). The MLUs of both types of speech samples contained peaks and valleys, these reflecting an inverse relation such that peaks in crib-speech MLU tended to correspond with dips in social-context speech MLU, and vice versa.

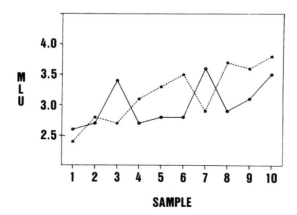

Figure 3-6. Crib-speech and social-context-speech MLUs for Child F. Solid line indicates crib-speech MLU. Dashed line indicates social-context-speech MLU.

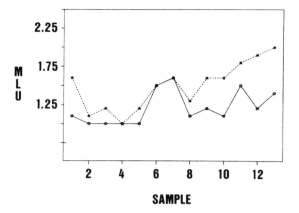

Figure 3-7. Crib-speech and social-context-speech MLUs for Child G. Solid line indicates crib-speech MLU. Dashed line indicates social-context-speech MLU.

Child G

The MLUs for Child G exhibited the peaks and dips common to all of the children discussed to this point (Figure 3-7). However, there was not an inverse relation between these peaks and valleys for crib-speech and social-context-speech MLUs. Child G was similar to Child E in that the peaks of crib-speech MLU corresponded to the peaks of social-context-speech MLU (with the exception of the next to last sample). The same held true for the dips in MLU in both types of speech sample. Crib-speech MLU was usually lower than social-context-speech MLU.

Child H

The crib-speech and social-context-speech MLUs for Child H did not vary consistently relative to one another (Figure 3-8). Instead, crib-speech MLU was some-

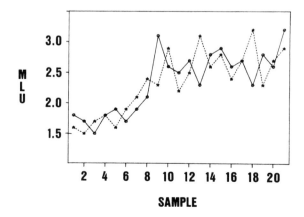

Figure 3-8. Crib-speech and social-context-speech MLUs for Child H. Solid line indicates crib-speech MLU. Dashed line indicates social-context-speech MLU.

times higher and sometimes lower than social-context-speech MLU. The MLUs of both types of speech contained peaks and valleys. The peaks and valleys of the two types of speech samples exhibited an inverse relation on several occasions. On other occasions, dips in MLU occurred for both crib speech and social-context speech, the same sometimes being true for increases in MLU.

Child I

In the first two samples, crib-speech MLU was higher than social-context-speech MLU (Figure 3-9). From then on, social-context-speech MLU was higher than crib-speech MLU. The MLUs of both speech types contained peaks and valleys, although the peaks and valleys were more pronounced for crib speech. The inverse relation for peaks and valleys for the two speech types held for some of the samples but not for others, where the MLUs of the two speech types rose or fell together.

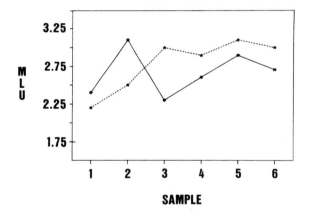

Figure 3-9. Crib-speech and social-context-speech MLUs for Child I. Solid line indicates crib-speech MLU. Dashed line indicates social-context-speech MLU.

Child J

The social-context-speech MLUs were almost always higher than those for crib speech (Figure 3-10). The MLUs of both types of speech contained peaks and valleys, with crib-speech MLU being more variable than social-context-speech MLU. Although there were samples in which an inverse relation held for a peak of one speech type MLU and a dip for the other speech type MLU, the MLUs of the two speech types were more likely to rise or fall together.

Child K

Neither type of speech had consistently higher MLUs than the other (Figure 3-11). There were many peaks and valleys in both types of speech samples. On occasions these peaks and valleys exhibited an inverse relation. More often, the MLUs of the two speech types rose or fell together.

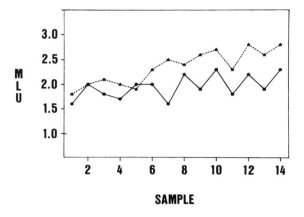

Figure 3-10. Crib-speech and social-context-speech MLUs for Child J. Solid line indicates crib-speech MLU. Dashed line indicates social-context-speech MLU.

Child L

Neither type of speech sample consistently had higher MLUs than the other, although the peaks of crib-speech MLU were higher than those of social-context-speech MLU (Figure 3-12). Similarly, the sudden declines in crib-speech MLU were much more dramatic than those of social-context speech. The peaks and valleys did not tend to reflect opposite tendencies for the two types of speech samples, but instead reflected considerable change in crib-speech MLU, social-context-speech MLU varying much less dramatically.

Child M

Neither type of speech sample was consistently higher or lower than the other (Figure 3-13). The MLUs of both types of speech samples contained peaks and

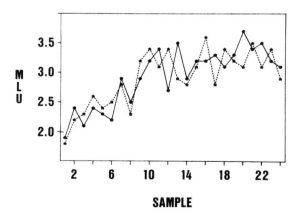

Figure 3-11. Crib-speech and social-context-speech MLUs for Child K. Solid line indicates crib-speech MLU. Dashed line indicates social-context-speech MLU.

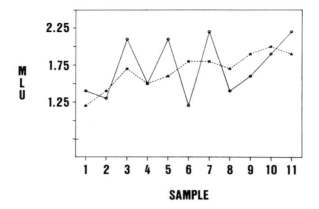

Figure 3-12. Crib-speech and social-context-speech MLUs for Child L. Solid line indicates crib-speech MLU. Dashed line indicates social-context-speech MLU.

valleys. The peaks and valleys sometimes coincided but also sometimes exhibited an inverse relation. Once again, crib-speech MLU varied much more than social-context-speech MLU.

Child N

Social-context-speech MLU was almost always higher than crib-speech MLU, although the most dramatic peak was in the crib-speech samples. (Figure 3-14). This was also a case in which crib-speech MLU did not exceed social-context-speech MLU. The MLUs of both speech types contained many peaks and valleys, although they seemed to be more drastic in the crib-speech samples. The peaks and valleys for the two speech samples tended to coincide rather than vary inversely.

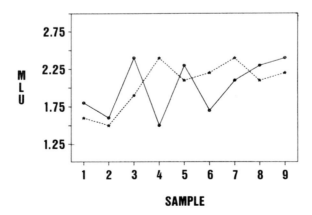

Figure 3-13. Crib-speech and social-context-speech MLUs for Child M. Solid line indicates crib-speech MLU. Dashed line indicates social-context-speech MLU.

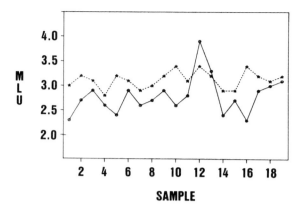

Figure 3-14. Crib-speech and social-context-speech MLUs for Child N. Solid line indicates crib-speech MLU. Dashed line indicates social-context-speech MLU.

Summary of Individual MLU Analyses

1. Four of the children had consistently higher MLUs for social-context speech than for crib speech. The opposite pattern held for three of the children. The remaining seven children did not exhibit any consistent pattern in regard to the MLUs of crib speech and social-context speech. In the speech samples obtained from these seven children, crib speech MLUs were occasionally higher than social-context speech MLUs, but the opposite pattern was also frequently observed.
2. Each of the children's MLUs exhibited peaks and valleys. Crib speech MLU peaks and valleys tended to be more drastic than was the case for social-context-speech MLU.
3. Ten of the children's MLUs reflected an inverse relation between the peaks and valleys of crib speech and those of social-context speech. When this relation was observed, a peak in MLU for one type of speech corresponded with a dip in MLU for the other type of speech. For the remaining four children, peaks in crib speech MLU tended to correspond with peaks in social-context speech MLU, the same being true for dips in MLU.

Discussion

It is clear from these results that there are considerable individual differences in the relation of crib-speech MLU to social-context-speech MLU. The MLU patterns suggest that crib speech and social-context speech are related in certain general ways in spite of these individual differences. Social-context-speech MLU tended to be more stable than crib-speech MLU. There were also many instances in which there was an inverse relation between the peaks and valleys of the two types of MLU. The

MLU analyses, then, imply that crib speech and social-context speech do differ in certain ways and that development in one speech setting is related to development in the other speech setting (to no one's surprise, I am sure—after all, it is the same child in both contexts). Still, it is important to remember that MLU provides a gross indication of grammatical development. The extent to which the observed MLU patterns correspond to patterns of linguistic practice will be one of the concerns of the next chapter. This will allow us to ascertain the significance of both the general MLU patterns and the individual differences in MLU patterns for patterns of linguistic practice.

4. Linguistic Practice

In this chapter, the data concerning the linguistic practice of the 14 subjects will be presented. Linguistic practice is defined here as those speech sequences constituting buildups, breakdowns, completions, substitutions, or exact reproductions (imitation or repetition). Sound play was excluded from these analyses. Only sequences involving words and word combinations were considered. Analyses based on group data will be presented first. This presentation will be followed by a discussion of the patterns exhibited by the individual children.

Group Analyses

Practice Type

The overall frequency of each type of practice will be considered first. These analyses combine the data from the crib-speech and social-context-speech samples. Exact reproductions were more frequent than buildups, $t(13) = 4.36$, $p < .01$; breakdowns, $t(13) = 3.72$, $p < .01$; completions, $t(13) = 4.49$, $p < .01$; and substitutions, $t(13) = 4.52$, $p < .01$. Breakdowns were more frequent than buildups, $t(13) = 2.94$, $p < .05$; completions, $t(13) = 3.80$, $p < .01$; and substitutions, $t(13) = 2.31$, $p < .05$. Buildups were more frequent than completions, $t(13) = 2.58$, $p < .05$. There were no other significant differences. In terms of overall absolute frequency, then, the five practice types may be rank ordered from most to least frequent as follows: exact reproductions, breakdowns, buildups, substitutions, and completions.

Speech Type

Another comparison involved the relative frequency of practice in crib speech and in social-context speech. These analyses combined the five types of practice. Overall, there were more instances of practice in social-context speech than in crib speech, $t(13) = 14.21$, $p < .001$. However, this was not the case for relative frequency. Relative frequency of practice in crib speech and in social-context speech was determined by dividing the total number of practice instances in one type of speech sample by the total number of utterances in the same speech-sampling situation (crib speech or social-context speech). In terms of relative frequency, practice was more common in crib speech than in social-context speech, $t(13) = 6.05$, $p < .001$. Thus, although practice was more frequent in social-context speech than in crib speech in terms of absolute numbers, practice comprised a greater proportion of crib speech than social-context speech.

The above comparisons involved crib speech and the combined three types of social-context speech situations. These three types are (a) social/self, in which the child provided the model for the subsequent practice instance and in which the child is engaged in some communicative activity; (b) social/other, in which another person provided the model for the child's subsequent practice behavior, and (c) asocial/self, in which the child provided the model but is not attempting to communicate with the present other person(s). The following analyses compared the four types of speech (crib speech and the three types of social-context speech). Overall, practice based on models produced by the self was more frequent than practice based on models produced by others, $t(13) = 11.12$, $p < .001$. Practice in crib speech was more frequent than practice in the social/self situation, $t(13) = 4.78$, $p < .001$; the social/other situation, $t(13) = 5.21$, $p < .001$; and the asocial/self situation, $t(13) = 6.25$, $p < .001$. Practice in the social/other situation was more frequent than practice in the social/self situation, $t(13) = 2.83$, $p < .05$, and the asocial/self situation, $t(13) = 3.04$, $p < .05$. Practice in the social/self situation was more common than practice in the asocial/self situation, $t(13) = 2.91$, $p < .05$. To summarize these analyses, practice was more frequent in crib speech (which is a self-model context), next most frequent in the social/other situation, next most frequent in the social/self situation, and least frequent in the asocial/self situation. These analyses suggest that the crib-speech situation is particularly conducive to practice, particularly in that the asocial/self situation, a situation somewhat like crib speech in that children are not concerned with the present others, had the least frequent amount of linguistic practice. It may be, then, that the mere presence of others inhibits practice (see Kuczaj, 1982b), and that it is the absence of others which makes crib speech a particularly fruitful situation for linguistic practice.

It is important to keep in mind the fact that the inhibiting effect of others on linguistic practice is relative rather than absolute. Practice was more likely to occur in crib speech than in any of the three social-context speech-model situations. These comparisons involve crib-speech practice and practice in each of the three social-context speech-model situations. This sort of comparison may seem peculiar in that the sampling would seem to favor crib speech in that it comprised 45-

minute speech samples, while other speech-model types came from social-context samples, the extent of each type of speech-model varying from sample to sample in the social-context speech samples. It may be unfair to compare from one type of 45-minute sample (crib speech) with three types of practice from a single other 45-minute sample (social-context speech). Recall that in terms of absolute numbers, practice was more likely to occur in social-context speech than in crib speech when the three types of social-context speech were combined. On the other hand, practice was more likely to occur in crib speech than in social-context speech in terms of relative frequency. The above analyses, although not based on equal sampling of each speech-model context, are not necessarily misleading in that practice varied from crib-speech sample to crib-speech sample, as well as within each of the three speech-model situations comprising social-context speech. I have compared crib-speech practice with practice in each of the three social-context speech types in order to determine the extent to which practice was found in each of the four speech-model types, this comparison being necessary to evaluate the developmental significance of crib speech in the language acquisition process.

Interactions

The analyses just given and the corresponding speculations have been based on comparisons which combined practice types. The following analyses were directed toward uncovering relations among model type, speech type, and practice type. The first set of analyses held practice type constant and varied speech-model type.

Buildups. There was no significant difference between buildups in crib speech and in social-context speech (combining the three types of social-context speech). However, buildups were more frequent in crib speech than in the social/self situation, $t(13) = 2.82$, $p < .05$, the social/other situation, $t(13) = 4.58$, $p < .01$, and the asocial/other situation, $t(13) = 5.27$, $p < .001$. Buildups in the social/self situation were more frequent than buildups in the social/other situation, $t(13) = 2.28$, $p < .05$. Of the four speech/model situations, crib speech was most likely to yield buildups, the next most productive situation for buildups being the social/self situation. Buildups in crib speech seem most likely to serve the function of linguistic practice, as Weir (1962) suggested, while those in the social/self situation seem to serve a communicative function. In the social/self situation, children seem to use buildups to facilitate their communicative attempts, the result of a buildup being a more complete utterance that is more likely to result in accurate comprehension by the listener. Given this possibility, the consideration of practice type and speech-model type interactions becomes important, not only to determine how the interaction affects frequency of practice but also to determine better the reasons why each type of practice is likely or unlikely to occur in each situation.

Breakdowns. Breakdowns were more frequent in social-context speech (combining the three types) than in crib speech, $t(13) = 10.28$, $p < .001$. Breakdowns in the social/other situation were more frequent than breakdowns in crib speech,

$t(13) = 4.80$, $p < .001$; in the social/self situation, $t(13) = 6.53$, $p < .001$; or in the asocial/self situation, $t(13) = 7.23$, $p < .001$. Breakdowns were more frequent in crib speech than in the social/self situation, $t(13) = 3.19$, $p < .01$, or the asocial-self situation, $t(13) = 4.04$, $p < .01$. There was no significant difference between breakdowns in the social/self situation and the asocial/self situation. In summary, breakdowns were more frequent when another person provided the model, next most frequent in crib speech, and least frequent in the social/self and asocial/self situations.

Present others seem to provide young children with many utterances that children respond to with a breakdown (that is, an incomplete repetition of the other's utterance). Children are more likely to provide their own models for breakdowns in the crib-speech situation than in either the social/self or asocial/self situations. This pattern fits well with the notion that young children learn grammar from other's utterances, particularly if the children notice the mismatch between their broken-down version and the original utterance produced by another. This in turn might help children to learn to use breakdowns as a language-learning strategy, one in which children themselves provide the model and the subsequent breakdown, in order to discover structural regularities in language. The fact that children are more likely to use breakdowns in crib speech than in either of the other self-model situations also supports the notion that children use crib speech to practice linguistic forms they are in the process of acquiring.

Completions. There was no significant difference between completions in crib speech and in social-context speech (combining the three types of social-context speech). Completions were more frequent in crib speech than in the social/other situation, $t(13) = 3.36$, $p < .01$, or in the asocial/self situation, $t(13) = 2.81$, $p < .05$. Completions in the social/self situation were more frequent than were completions in the social/other situation, $t(13) = 2.86$, $p < .05$. The frequency of completions in each of the speech-model situations may be ordered from most to least frequent as follows: crib, social/self, asocial/self, and social/other. Children were most likely to use completions in crib speech and in the social-context situation in which the children provided the model utterance to be completed. The greater frequency of completions in crib speech than in any other type of speech-model situation again supports the notion that crib speech is an optimal situation for linguistic practice, while the use of completions in the social/self situation seems more likely to serve a communicative function. Completing an utterance in a social setting typically increases the likelihood that the utterance will be accurately comprehended by the listener. Children were unlikely to complete the utterance of another speaker for two reasons: (a) children were less competent English speakers than the adults, and (b) the adults rarely provided children with an opportunity to complete one of their (the adults') utterances.

Substitutions. Substitutions were more frequent in social-context speech (combining the three types) than in crib speech, $t(13) = 3.12$, $p < .05$. However, substitutions were more frequent in the crib-speech situation than in the social/self situation, $t(13) = 2.34$, $p < .05$; the social/other situation, $t(13) = 4.82$, $p < .05$; or the social/self situation, $t(13) = 2.92$, $p < .05$. There were no other significant differences, although substitutions were somewhat more frequent in the social/self situation than in either the asocial/self or social/other situations. In the case of substitutions, as in the case of buildups and completions, models produced by the self were more likely to result in a practice behavior. Crib speech may be important in that it provides children with a situation in which they always provide the model.

Exact Reproductions. Exact reproductions were more frequent in social-context speech than in crib speech, $t(13) = 2.69$, $p < .05$. Exact reproductions in the social/self situation were more frequent than exact reproductions in crib speech, $t(13) = 2.41$, $p < .05$, or the asocial/self situation, $t(13) = 2.5$, $p < .05$. For exact reproductions, then, as for breakdowns, models produced by others were more likely to be followed by a practice behavior. The exact reproductions that occur in the social-self situation typically seem to reflect a communicative desire on the part of the child (usually one of emphasis).

The next set of analyses held speech/model type constant and varied practice type.

Crib Speech. Within the crib-speech setting, buildups were more frequent than breakdowns, $t(13) = 4.52$, $p < .01$, completions, $t(13) = 3.44$, $p < .01$, or substitutions, $t(13) = 2.25$, $p < .05$, but less frequent than exact reproductions, $t(13) = 2.4$, $p < .05$. Exact reproductions in crib speech were also more frequent than breakdowns, $t(13) = 3.29$, $p < .01$, completions, $t(13) = 3.69$, $p < .01$, or substitutions, $t(13) = 3.38$, $p < .01$. Within the crib-speech setting, then, the five types of practice may be ordered from most to least frequent as follows: exact reproductions, buildups, substitutions, completions, and breakdowns (the latter three *not* differing significantly). Exact reproductions, in general more likely to occur when another produced the model than when children produced the model (see previous paragraph), were nonetheless the most frequent type of practice in crib speech, a self/model situation. This finding aptly illustrates the pervasiveness of exact reproductions as a form of linguistic practice and would seem to suggest that this type of imitation and repetition serves some important function for the language-learning child, even though we have yet to ascertain the exact nature of this function. It seems unlikely that children would engage in a behavior to such an extent if the behavior was truly valueless (recall that there are individual differences in the extent to which children do imitate or repeat, Bloom et al., 1974). Given that this surge of exact reproductions occurs in the age range during which children learn a considerable amount of language, exact reproductions may in fact function as a language-learning device. Precisely how this is so is yet to be determined.

Social/Self. Within the social/self situation, exact reproductions were more frequent than buildups, $t(13) = 3.30$, $p < .01$; breakdowns, $t(13) = 6.07$, $p < .001$; completions, $t(13) = 3.37$, $p < .01$, and substitutions, $t(13) = 3.63$, $p < .01$. The only other significant effects concerned breakdowns. Buildups were more frequent than breakdowns, $t(13) = 3.64$, $p < .01$. Completions were more frequent than breakdowns, $t(13) = 2.32$, $p < .05$. Substitutions were more frequent than breakdowns, $t(13) = 4.01$, $p < .01$. The overall frequency of the five practice types in the social/self setting was as follows (from most to least frequent): exact reproductions, buildups, substitutions, completions, and breakdowns. This pattern is identical to that for the crib-speech situation, another in which the children provide their own model utterances.

Social/Other. Exact reproductions were more frequent than buildups, $t(13) = 4.19$, $p < .01$; breakdowns, $t(13) = 4.52$, $p < .01$; and substitutions, $t(13) = 3.53$, $p < .01$. Breakdowns were more frequent than buildups, $t(13) = 7.01$, $p < .001$; completions, $t(13) = 6.84$, $p < .001$; and substitutions, $t(13) = 6.43$, $p < .001$. There were no other significant differences. In this situation in which another provides the model, children are most likely to respond with an exact reproduction or a breakdown. The lack of a significant difference between exact reproductions and breakdowns undoubtedly reflects the complexity of the model. Young children cannot exactly reproduce model utterances beyond their competence, but are likely to hear many utterances that are beyond their competence. Whether children respond with an exact imitation or a breakdown seems more likely to rest on the complexity of the model utterance than on a decision on the child's part, particularly in the early phases of grammatical development. Later, when children become more competent both linguistically and representationally (imitation and repetition), they become better able to decide if they will reproduce something exactly or partially. Thus, early on in the language-learning process, children are more likely to imitate exactly short utterances and more likely to break down long utterances (that is, repeat a part of them). This pattern seems to hold throughout the age range studied in the present investigation.

Summary. The numerical data upon which the above analyses are based are summarized in Table 4-1. The rank orders of the five practice types within each speech-model situation are summarized in Tables 4-2 and 4-3. These tables, although simply summarizing the analysis discussed previously, document several group trends. Exact reproductions were the dominant type of linguistic practice. Crib speech was the

Table 4-1. Total Number of Instances of Each Practice Type in Each Speech-Model Situation

Practice Type	Speech-Model Type			
	Crib	Social/Self	Asocial/Self	Social/Other
Buildups	1449	673	277	282
Breakdowns	830	240	279	2306
Completions	835	497	205	210
Exact reproductions	1619	2367	1602	2454
Substitutions	926	522	337	347

Table 4-2. Rank Order of the Frequency of the Five Practice Types (from most to least frequent) in Each Speech-Model Situation

Speech-Model Type			
Crib	Social/Self	Asocial/Self	Social/Other
Exact reproductions	Exact reproductions	Exact reproductions	Exact reproductions
Buildups	Buildups	Substitutions	Breakdowns
Substitutions	Substitutions	Breakdowns	Substitutions
Completions	Completions	Buildups	Buildups
Breakdowns	Breakdowns	Completions	Completions

dominant type of speech-model situation in regard to linguistic practice. There were also practice type and speech-model type interactions. Buildups, completions, and substitutions were most frequent in crib speech, while breakdowns and exact reproductions were most common in the social/other situation. With the exception of breakdowns, the social/self situation was also a relatively fruitful source of linguistic practice. There were no statistically significant sex differences in regard to overall practice, practice type, or speech-model situation. All of these analyses reflect group data and group trends. In the following, we shall see if the patterns exhibited by individual children are consistent with these group patterns.

Preliminary Analyses of Individual Patterns

Table 4-4 shows the relative frequency of linguistic practice in crib speech and in social-context speech for each child. This comparison was made by combining the five types of linguistic practice found in a speech sampling situation for a child and dividing this by the number of utterances recorded in the speech-sampling situation for the child. The relative frequency of practice in social-context speech ranged

Table 4-3. Rank Order of Frequency (from most to least frequent) of the Four Speech-Model Situations for Each Type of Practice

Practice Type				
Buildups	Breakdowns	Completions	Exact Reproductions	Substitutions
Crib	Social/other	Crib	Social/other	Crib
Social/self	Crib	Social/self	Social/self	Social/self
Social/other	Asocial/self	Social/other	Crib	Social/other
Asocial/other	Social/self	Asocial/self	Asocial/self	Asocial/self

Table 4-4. Relative Frequency for Linguistic Practice in Each Type of Speech Sample for Each Child[a]

Child	Social-Context Speech	Crib Speech
A	34.9	49.5
B	21.2	38.7
C	49.3	53.8
D	30.2	37.4
E	28.7	46.7
F	23.4	41.0
G	26.8	32.5
H	41.3	63.8
I	16.5	41.6
J	22.1	48.4
K	32.3	57.6
L	29.4	35.1
M	19.4	33.4
N	41.3	35.7

[a]Determined by dividing the number of instances of practice by the total number of utterances for each type of speech sample.

from 16.5% to 49.3%. The relative frequency of practice in crib speech ranged from 32.5% to 63.8%. This initial comparison provides support for the notion that linguistic practice is more likely to occur in crib speech than in social-context speech, at least insofar as relative frequency is concerned. This hypothesis gains further support from the fact that 13 of the 14 children had higher relative frequencies of practice in crib speech than in social-context speech. The rank order of the children's relative frequency of practice in crib speech and the rank order of their relative frequency of practice in social-context speech proved to be statistically significant ($r(14) = .56$, $p < .05$). Children who are likely to produce linguistic practice in one context are also likely to do so in the other context.

Table 4-5 shows the relative frequency of the five types of linguistic practice for each child. These relative frequencies were determined by dividing the total number of instances of one type of practice (e.g., buildups) for a child by the total number of instances of practice for that child. Buildups ranged in relative frequency from 4.3% to 29.2%. Breakdowns ranged in relative frequency from 11.8% to 45.5%. Completions ranged in relative frequency from .1% to 19.5%. Substitutions ranged in relative frequency from 3.6% to 27.7%. Exact reproductions ranged in relative frequency from 22.8% to 76.5%. There are individual differences in the rank order of each of the practice types.

Another way to consider the data is to look at each child's use of linguistic practice in each of four speech-model situations. Table 4-6 shows the relative fre-

Table 4-5. Relative Frequency of Each Type of Linguistic Practice[a]

	Practice Type				
Child	Buildup	Breakdown	Completion	Substitution	Exact Reproduction
A	29.2	15.3	.4	27.7	27.4
B	21.3	18.6	17.6	12.1	30.3
C	11.7	12.8	2.8	9.3	63.5
D	11.6	29.3	6.4	12.8	39.9
E	10.8	18.2	19.5	10.6	40.2
F	15.9	16.7	10.6	11.0	45.7
G	4.3	45.5	1.1	3.6	45.5
H	11.6	20.7	8.3	5.8	53.6
I	12.3	13.5	6.2	15.3	52.6
J	6.2	11.8	.3	5.2	76.5
K	21.6	14.5	11.3	10.4	42.1
L	10.2	18.1	9.7	11.4	50.6
M	26.6	30.9	8.2	11.5	22.8
N	28.2	16.5	.1	9.4	45.8

[a]Determined by dividing the number of instances of one type of practice by the total number of practice instances for that child.

Table 4-6. Relative Frequency of Buildups in Each of the Four Speech-Model Situations for Each Child[a]

	Situation Type			
Child	Crib	Social/Self	Asocial/Self	Social/Other
A	59.3	26.4	.2	14.1
B	65.1	19.4	9.1	6.4
C	46.7	43.9	5.0	4.4
D	28.9	30.4	31.9	8.7
E	23.9	53.5	8.8	13.8
F	61.5	19.3	5.3	13.9
G	56.3	25.0	12.5	6.2
H	62.2	3.2	18.1	16.1
I	34.4	22.6	41.9	1.1
J	35.6	53.4	5.5	5.5
K	69.7	12.1	5.7	12.6
L	63.0	10.9	6.9	19.1
M	71.5	21.8	3.9	2.9
N	52.3	38.2	1.1	8.3

[a]Determined by dividing the number of buildups in each situation by the total number of buildups for that child.

quency of buildups in each of the speech-model contexts for each child. The range of relative frequencies of buildups in each of the four situations was as follows: crib—23.9% to 71.5%; social/self—3.2% to 53.5%; asocial/self—.2% to 41.9%; social/other—1.1% to 19.1%. Children are most likely to build up their own utterances, and are most likely to do so in the crib-speech situation. They are unlikely to build on other's utterances, most likely due to their lack of productive language skills.

Table 4-7 shows the relative frequencies of breakdowns in each of the four situations for each child. The range of relative frequencies for breakdowns for the sample as a whole was from 4.5% to 48.5% in crib speech, 1.6% to 21.5% in the social/self situation, .6% to 9.7% in the asocial/self situation, and 30.2% to 91.4% in the social/other situation. This pattern is different than that observed for buildups. For breakdowns, the most common situation is that in which another person provides the model that the child subsequently breaks down. As noted earlier, the fact that children are more likely to respond to another's utterance than to their own utterances with a breakdown has to do with the greater linguistic competence of others in comparison to young children. If young children attempt to repeat what they hear, partial success is the most likely occurrence. This does not mean that breakdowns are an insignificant practice type for the young child. Partial reproduction is more likely to aid memory and thereby acquisition, than no reproduction. Moreover, it is possible that children learn to break down their own utterances from their breakdowns of others' utterances. If so, parents might not model breakdowns (i.e., actually engage in breakdowns) for children, but might indirectly facilitate children's use of breakdowns when the children provide the models by initially providing children with model utterances to break down. This possibility will be considered in the next chapter.

Table 4-8 shows the relative frequencies of completions in the four target situations for each child. The relative frequencies of completions ranged from zero to 78.7% in the crib-speech situation, 7.2% to 75% in the social/self situation, zero to 37.5% in the asocial/self situation, and zero to 39.2% in the social/other situation. Children were more likely to complete their own utterances than to complete those of others.

Table 4-9 shows the relative frequencies of substitutions in the four target-situation types for each child. The range of relative frequencies of substitutions for each type of situation for the sample as a whole was as follows: crib—11.1% to 66.4%; social/self—2.9% to 56.5%; asocial/self—4.8% to 44.4%; social/other—1.3% to 56.3%. In general, children were more likely to engage in substitutions when they provided the model than when another provided the model.

Table 4-10 shows the relative frequencies of exact reproductions in each of the four target situations for each child. The range of relative frequencies of exact reproductions in each of the target situations was as follows: crib—18.0% to 48.7%; social/self—7.5% to 34.6%; asocial/self—8.3% to 41.2%; social/other—3.9% to 41.9%. Once again, children seemed more likely to engage in exact reproductions when they had produced the model than when someone else had produced the model.

Table 4-7. Relative Frequency of Breakdowns in Each of the Four Speech-Model Situations for Each Child[a]

Child	Situation Type			
	Crib	Social/Self	Asocial/Self	Social/Other
A	48.5	16.8	4.4	30.2
B	15.9	11.3	5.9	66.9
C	4.5	4.4	.6	90.3
D	4.6	2.3	1.7	91.4
E	17.1	13.5	9.2	60.2
F	34.9	3.9	.7	60.4
G	4.7	1.8	2.4	91.1
H	29.4	1.9	9.7	58.9
I	5.9	1.9	2.9	89.3
J	15.8	21.6	1.4	61.2
K	41.4	1.8	7.7	49.1
L	14.7	1.6	2.3	81.5
M	31.3	3.8	5.3	59.6
N	40.3	16.8	.6	42.3

[a]Determined by dividing the number of breakdowns for each situation by the total number of breakdowns for each child.

Table 4-8. Relative Frequency of Completions in Each of the Four Speech-Model Situations[a]

Child	Situation Type			
	Crib	Social/Self	Asocial/Self	Social/Other
A	26.4	50.9	14.3	0
B	56.7	30.1	12.6	.6
C	32.3	40.3	12.9	14.5
D	10.5	34.2	26.3	29.0
E	32.1	17.5	11.2	29.2
F	65.0	21.5	3.3	10.2
G	12.5	12.5	37.5	37.5
H	78.7	7.2	12.9	1.2
I	27.7	23.4	27.2	21.7
J	0	75.0	0	25.0
K	38.0	30.2	17.6	14.2
L	42.0	21.7	21.7	14.7
M	29.1	54.5	9.1	7.3
N	55.2	36.6	8.3	0

[a]Determined by dividing the number of completions in each situation type by the total number of completions for each child.

Table 4-9. Relative Frequency of Substitution in Each of the Four
Speech-Model Situations[a]

		Situation Type		
Child	Crib	Social/Self	Asocial/Self	Social/Other
A	52.6	34.2	9.5	3.7
B	66.3	12.2	16.3	5.2
C	28.9	56.5	9.2	5.4
D	53.9	14.5	30.3	1.3
E	40.4	15.1	29.5	15.1
F	53.3	18.3	10.0	18.3
G	11.1	33.3	44.4	11.2
H	31.2	2.9	9.6	56.3
I	66.4	6.9	14.7	12.0
J	40.3	33.9	4.8	20.9
K	63.8	11.9	9.8	14.5
L	59.3	17.3	9.9	13.5
M	66.2	10.4	10.4	13.0
N	41.2	40.3	13.7	4.8

[a]Determined by dividing the number of substitutions in a situation type by
the total number of substitutions for each child.

Table 4-10. Relative Frequency of Exact Reproductions in Each of
the Four Speech-Model Situations[a]

		Situation Type		
Child	Crib	Social/Self	Asocial/Self	Social/Other
A	22.5	19.2	41.2	17.1
B	34.9	16.3	25.2	23.6
C	28.4	25.6	12.3	33.7
D	40.1	20.3	16.5	23.2
E	37.6	17.2	22.1	23.1
F	26.5	29.8	16.7	27.0
G	28.3	25.9	8.3	37.5
H	22.3	28.2	24.9	24.6
I	34.7	20.9	14.6	29.8
J	48.7	36.6	10.8	3.9
K	19.6	28.8	9.8	41.9
L	18.0	7.5	32.7	41.7
M	33.9	34.6	8.5	23.0
N	30.2	26.3	17.4	26.1

[a]Determined by dividing the number of exact reproductions in each situation
by the total number of exact reproductions for each child.

More Analyses of the Linguistic Practice
of Individual Children

The analyses just presented have focused on general patterns of linguistic practice in the data obtained from the 14 children. The following analyses serve two
functions. First, they reveal the extent to which the general patterns hold true for
each child. Second, they specify the extent of individual differences.

The initial discussion of the practice patterns exhibited by individual children
will focus on five comparisons. First, the overall absolute frequency of each of the
five practice types will be ranked from most to least frequent for those practice
instances in which the model utterance was produced by the child (combining the
crib-speech data and two of the three social-context-speech types) and those in
which the model utterance was produced by another (social-context speech only).
This comparison provides a rough means of specifying which practice type was
most common when the child produced the model as opposed to when another person produced the model.

The second comparison concerns the total number of instances of each practice
type for each child when the model was produced by the child or by another. This
comparison specifies whether self-models or other-models were most common for
each type of practice and the extent of the differences (in terms of total numbers).
This information complements that of the first comparison.

The third comparison focuses on the three types of self-models: (a) those produced in crib speech (crib), (b) those produced in social-context speech that seemed
to have some communicative intent (social), and (c) those produced in social-
context speech but that did not seem to have any communication intent (asocial).
This comparison is a critical one in that it makes possible the comparison of crib
speech with other self-model situations, which in turn helps to determine the
developmental significance of crib speech as a self-model situation.

The fourth comparison rank orders the absolute frequency of each practice type
in crib speech and in social-context speech (combining the three types of social-
context speech). This comparison complements the comparisons given previously in
that it specifies similarities and differences in the linguistic practice each child produced in crib speech and in social-context speech.

The final comparison focuses on the total number of instances of each practice
type observed in crib speech and in social-context speech (combining the three
types of social-context speech types). This comparison further resolves the issue of
the relative importance of crib speech and social-context speech in regard to linguistic practice. In order to present a more general picture of the practice patterns
exhibited by individual children, each of the five sets of comparisons will be presented for each child, followed by a general discussion of these patterns.

Child A

Child A was most likely to engage in the types of linguistic practice of concern
when he provided the model utterance on which the practice was based (Table
4-11). This was true for each type of practice. However, there were differences in

Table 4-11. Comparison of Each Practice Type When Produced
Following a Self-Model or an Other-Model (Child A)

Practice Type	Most Common with Self-Model or Other-Model	Absolute Numbers (self-other)
Buildups	Self	170-29
Breakdowns	Self	127-56
Completions	Self	220-0
Exact reproductions	Self	230-48
Substitutions	Self	46-2

the rank order of practice types in self-model and other-model contexts (Table 4-12). Completions were second most frequent in the self-model context, but least frequent in the other-model context. This most likely reflects the fact that others rarely provided Child A with utterances that he could complete. Breakdowns, fourth in absolute frequency in the self-model situation, were first in the other-model situation, reflecting Child A's tendency to provide partial imitations of other's utterances. These findings support the notion that the processes involved in practice based on self-models and practice based on other-models may be quite different. In the former, the child is altering his own previous utterance. In the latter, he is altering another's utterance. This difference seemingly affects the probability of occurrence of each type of linguistic practice.

Table 4-13 shows that within the context of practice based on self-models, crib speech seemed to be an important context for the occurrence of such practice. Buildups, breakdowns, and substitutions were most common in crib speech. Completions were most common in social speech. Exact repetitions were most frequent in asocial speech. For Child A, crib speech seemed to be the most likely place to produce linguistic practice, with social and asocial speech playing somewhat less important roles in this regard. This conclusion, based on comparisons of self-model practice instances, is somewhat misleading. Combining the instances of linguistic practice in the three social-context speech types and comparing this total with that

Table 4-12. Rank Order of Absolute Frequencies (from most to least frequent) of Each Practice Type When the Model Was Produced by the Self or by Another (Child A)

Model	
Self	Other
Exact reproductions	Breakdowns
Completions	Exact reproductions
Buildups	Buildups
Breakdowns	Substitutions
Substitutions	Completions

Table 4-13. Rank Order of Each Practice Type in Each of the Three Self-Model Situations (Child A)

Practice Type	Most Frequent[a]	Next Most Frequent[a]	Least Frequent[a]
Buildups	Crib (119)	Social (42)	Asocial (9)
Breakdowns	Crib (75)	Asocial (28)	Social (24)
Completions	Social (112)	Crib (85)	Asocial (0)
Exact reproductions	Asocial (114)	Crib (63)	Social (53)
Substitutions	Crib (25)	Social (16)	Asocial (5)

[a]Numbers in parentheses indicate the number of instances of each practice type in each of the three situations.

Table 4-14. Comparison of Each Type of Practice in Crib Speech and Social-Context Speech (Child A)

Practice Type	Most Common in Crib or Social-Context	Absolute Numbers (crib-social)
Buildups	Crib	119-30
Breakdowns	Social	75-108
Completions	Social	85-135
Exact reproductions	Social	63-215
Substitutions	Crib	25-23

exhibited in crib speech shows that buildups and substitutions were in fact more common in crib speech, but that breakdowns, completions, and exact repetitions were more common in social-context speech (Table 4-14). Thus, crib speech was an important type of self-model practice situation for Child A, but the social-context situation also was important. The rank order of practice types for crib speech showed that crib speech contained relatively many buildups. The rank order of practice types for social-context speech contained relatively many exact reproductions (Table 4-15). Completions, breakdowns, and substitutions held the same

Table 4-15. Rank Order of Absolute Frequency (from most to least frequent) of Each Type of Practice in Crib Speech and in Social-Context Speech (Child A)

Speech Type	
Crib	Social-Context
Buildups	Exact reproductions
Completions	Completions
Breakdowns	Breakdowns
Exact reproductions	Buildups
Substitutions	Substitutions

Table 4-16. Comparison of Each Practice Type When Produced Following a Self-Model or an Other-Model (Child B)

Practice Type	Most Common with Self-Model or Other-Model	Absolute Numbers (self-other)
Buildups	Self	164-9
Breakdowns	Other	50-101
Completions	Self	142-1
Exact reproductions	Self	188-58
Substitutions	Self	93-5

rank order positions in crib speech and in social-context speech, although the number of instances of each of these practice types differed in the two speech contexts (the difference was minimal for substitutions).

Child B

With the exception of breakdowns, Child B was more likely to engage in each type of linguistic practice when he had produced the model utterance than when another person had produced the original utterance (Table 4-16). Moreover, break-downs were the most frequent type of linguistic practice produced in response to a model produced by another but the least frequent type of linguistic practice when Child B had produced the model (Table 4-17). Completions were the third most frequent type of linguistic practice produced in response to a self-model but the least frequent type of practice to occur in response to a model produced by another (Table 4-17). Of the three self-model situations, crib speech was the context most likely to yield each type of practice. Buildups, breakdowns, and completions were more common in the social-speech context than the asocial-speech context, the opposite pattern holding for exact reproductions and substitutions (Table 4-18).

Crib speech also proved to be an important context for linguistic practice when compared to the combined types of social-context speech (Table 4-19). Buildups, completions, and substitutions were more common in crib speech than in social-

Table 4-17. Rank Order of Absolute Frequencies (from most to least frequent) of Each Practice Type When the Model Was Produced by the Self or by Another (Child B)

Model	
Self	Other
Exact reproductions	Breakdowns
Buildups	Exact reproductions
Completions	Buildups
Substitutions	Substitutions
Breakdowns	Completions

Table 4-18. Rank Order of Each Practice Type in Each of the Three Self-Model Situations (Child B)

Practice Type	Most Frequent[a]	Next Most Frequent[a]	Least Frequent[a]
Buildups	Crib (114)	Social (34)	Asocial (16)
Breakdowns	Crib (24)	Social (17)	Asocial (9)
Completions	Crib (81)	Social (43)	Asocial (18)
Exact reproductions	Crib (86)	Asocial (62)	Social (40)
Substitutions	Crib (65)	Asocial (16)	Social (12)

[a]Numbers in parentheses indicate the number of instances of each practice type in each of the three situations.

Table 4-19. Comparison of Each Type of Practice in Crib Speech and Social-Context Speech (Child B)

Practice Type	Most Common in Crib or Social-Context	Absolute Numbers (crib-social)
Buildups	Crib	114-59
Breakdowns	Social	24-127
Completions	Crib	81-45
Exact reproductions	Social	86-160
Substitutions	Crib	65-33

context speech, whereas breakdowns and exact reproductions were more common in social-context speech than in crib speech. For Child B, then, there was an inter-action between type of linguistic practice and speech type (crib vs. social). This interaction was also evident in the rank orders shown in Table 4-20. Buildups were the most common type of practice in crib speech, but next to last in absolute frequency in social-context speech. Breakdowns, the least frequent type of practice in crib speech, were the second most frequent types of practice in social-context speech.

Table 4-20. Rank Order of Absolute Frequency (from most to least frequent) of Each Type of Practice in Crib Speech and in Social-Context Speech (Child B)

Speech Type	
Crib	Social-Context
Buildups	Exact reproductions
Exact reproductions	Breakdowns
Completions	Completions
Substitutions	Buildups
Breakdowns	Substitutions

Child C

With the exception of breakdowns, Child C was most likely to produce each type of practice when he produced the model (Table 4-21). Breakdowns were the least frequent type of practice when the model was self-produced, but were the second most frequent type of practice when another produced the model (Table 4-22). Child C was more likely to produce buildups and exact reproductions in crib speech than in either of the other self-model situations (Table 4-23). Completions and sub-

Table 4-21. Comparison of Each Practice Type When Produced Following a Self-Model or an Other-Model (Child C)

Practice Type	Most Common with Self-Model or Other-Model	Absolute Numbers (self-other)
Buildups	Self	239-22
Breakdowns	Other	28-259
Completions	Self	53-9
Exact reproductions	Self	941-478
Substitutions	Self	196-11

Table 4-22. Rank Order of Absolute Frequencies (from most to least frequent) of Each Practice Type When the Model Was Produced by the Self or by Another (Child C)

Model	
Self	Other
Exact reproductions	Exact reproductions
Buildups	Breakdowns
Substitutions	Buildups
Completions	Substitutions
Breakdowns	Completions

Table 4-23. Rank Order of Absolute Frequency (from most to least frequent) of Each Type of Practice in Crib Speech and in Social-Context Speech (Child C)

Speech Type	
Crib	Social-Context
Exact reproductions	Exact reproductions
Buildups	Breakdowns
Substitutions	Buildups
Completions	Substitutions
Breakdowns	Completions

Table 4-24. Rank Order of Each Practice Type in Each of the Three Self-Model Situations (Child C)

Practice Type	Most Frequent[a]	Next Most Frequent[a]	Least Frequent[a]
Buildups	Crib (122)	Social (105)	Asocial (12)
Breakdowns	Crib/Social (12 each)		Asocial (2)
Completions	Social (25)	Crib (20)	Asocial (8)
Exact reproductions	Crib (403)	Social (364)	Asocial (174)
Substitutions	Social (117)	Crib (60)	Asocial (19)

[a]Numbers in parentheses indicate the number of instances of each practice type in each of the three situations.

Table 4-25. Comparison of Each Type of Practice in Crib Speech and Social-Context Speech (Child C)

Practice Type	Most Common in Crib or Social-Context	Absolute Numbers (crib-social)
Buildups	Social	122-139
Breakdowns	Social	13-274
Completions	Social	20-42
Exact reproductions	Social	403-1016
Substitutions	Social	60-147

stitutions were more likely to be produced in social speech than in crib speech or asocial speech. The asocial speech setting was the self-model situation least likely to yield each of the practice types. Breakdowns once again provided a significant difference in regard to the rank order of the practice types in crib speech and in social-context speech (Table 4-24). Breakdowns were the least frequent type of practice in crib speech but the second most frequent type of practice in social-context speech. In terms of absolute frequency, each type of practice was more likely to occur in social-context speech than in crib speech (Table 4-25).

Child D

Buildups, completions, exact reproductions, and substitutions were more common when Child D produced the model than when another person produced the model. On the other hand, breakdowns were more likely to occur when another person produced the model than when Child D produced the model (Table 4-26). Breakdowns were once again the least frequent type of practice to result from a self-model, but the most frequent type of model to result from a model produced by another (Table 4-27). Buildups were the third most frequent type of practice to occur when Child D produced the original utterance, but the least frequent type of practice to occur when another person had produced the model (Table 4-27).

Breakdowns, exact repetitions, and substitutions were more common in crib speech than in either other type of self-model context (Table 4-28). Buildups were

Table 4-26. Comparison of Each Practice Type When Produced
Following a Self-Model or an Other-Model (Child D)

Practice Type	Most Common with Self-Model or Other-Model	Absolute Numbers (self-other)
Buildups	Self	63-6
Breakdowns	Other	15-159
Completions	Self	27-11
Exact reproductions	Self	192-45
Substitutions	Self	65-11

Table 4-27. Rank Order of Absolute Frequencies (from most to least frequent) of Each Practice Type When the Model Was Produced by the Self or by Another (Child D)

Model	
Self	Other
Exact reproductions	Breakdowns
Substitutions	Exact reproductions
Buildups	Completions / Substitutions tie
Completions	
Breakdowns	Buildups

more commonly produced in asocial speech than in crib speech or social speech. Completions were most frequently produced in social speech. Completions were least frequently produced in crib speech, as, somewhat surprisingly, were buildups. Crib speech seemed to be a less important practice context for Child D than for Child A, Child B, and Child C, especially for buildups and completions.

Each type of practice was produced more often in social-context speech than in crib speech (Table 4-29). However, there was an interaction between speech type

Table 4-28. Rank Order of Each Practice Type in Each of the Three Self-Model Situations (Child D)

Practice Type	Most Frequent[a]	Next Most Frequent[a]	Least Frequent[a]
Buildups	Asocial (22)	Social (21)	Crib (20)
Breakdowns	Crib (8)	Social (4)	Asocial (3)
Completions	Social (13)	Asocial (10)	Crib (4)
Exact reproductions	Crib (95)	Social (48)	Asocial (39)
Substitutions	Crib (41)	Asocial (23)	Social (11)

[a]Numbers in parentheses indicate the number of instances of each practice type in each of the three situations.

Table 4-29. Comparison of Each Type of Practice in Crib Speech and Social-Context Speech (Child D)

Practice Type	Most Common in Crib or Social-Context	Absolute Numbers (crib-social)
Buildups	Social	20-49
Breakdowns	Social	8-166
Completions	Social	4-34
Exact reproductions	Social	95-132
Substitutions	Social	41-45

Table 4-30. Rank Order of Absolute Frequency (from most to least frequent) of Each Type of Practice in Crib Speech and in Social-Context Speech (Child D)

Speech Type	
Crib	Social-Context
Exact reproductions	Breakdowns
Substitutions	Exact reproductions
Buildups	Buildups
Breakdowns	Substitutions
Completions	Completions

and practice type (Table 4-30). Breakdowns, fourth in frequency in crib speech, were the most frequent type of practice in social-context speech. Substitutions were the second most frequent type of practice in crib speech but fourth most frequent in social-context speech.

Child E

Once again, with the exception of breakdowns, each type of practice was more likely to occur following self-models than other-models (Table 4-31). Nonetheless, there was an interaction between type of model and type of practice (Table 4-32).

Table 4-31. Comparison of Each Practice Type When Produced Following a Self-Model or an Other-Model (Child E)

Practice Type	Most Common with Self-Model or Other-Model	Absolute Numbers (self-other)
Buildups	Self	145-14
Breakdowns	Other	100-151
Completions	Self	163-105
Exact reproductions	Self	425-128
Substitutions	Self	124-22

Table 4-32. Rank Order of Absolute Frequencies (from most to least frequent) of Each Practice Type When the Model Was Produced by the Self or by Another (Child E)

Model	
Self	Other
Exact reproductions	Breakdowns
Completions	Exact reproductions
Buildups	Completions
Substitutions	Substitutions
Breakdowns	Buildups

Breakdowns were the least frequent type of practice for self-models, but the most frequent type of practice for other models. Buildups, the third most frequent type of practice for self-models, were the least frequent type of practice when another person produced the model.

Breakdowns, completions, exact repetitions, and substitutions were more likely to occur in crib speech than in either other type of self-model speech context (Table 4-33). Buildups were produced more often in social speech than in crib speech or in asocial speech, and next most often in crib speech. Crib speech, then,

Table 4-33. Rank Order of Each Practice Type in Each of the Three Self-Model Situations (Child E)

Practice Type	Most Frequent[a]	Next Most Frequent[a]	Least Frequent[a]
Buildups	Social (85)	Crib (38)	Asocial (22)
Breakdowns	Crib (43)	Social (34)	Asocial (23)
Completions	Crib (86)	Asocial (47)	Social (30)
Exact reproductions	Crib (208)	Asocial (122)	Social (95)
Substitutions	Crib (95)	Asocial (43)	Social (22)

[a]Numbers in parentheses indicate the number of instances of each practice type in each of the three situations.

Table 4-34. Comparison of Each Type of Practice in Crib Speech and Social-Context Speech (Child E)

Practice Type	Most Common in Crib or Social-Context	Absolute Numbers (crib-social)
Buildups	Social	38-121
Breakdowns	Social	43-208
Completions	Social	86-182
Exact reproductions	Social	208-182
Substitutions	Social	59-87

Table 4-35. Rank Order of Absolute Frequency (from most to least frequent) of Each Type of Practice in Crib Speech and in Social-Context Speech (Child E)

Speech Type	
Crib	Social-Context
Exact reproductions	Exact reproductions
Completions	Breakdowns
Substitutions	Completions
Breakdowns	Buildups
Buildups	Substitutions

seemed to be an important context for linguistic practice for Child E, at least insofar as practice based on self-models was concerned.

Each type of practice was more likely to be produced in social-context speech than in crib speech (Table 4-34), although there was an interaction between practice type and speech type (Table 4-35). Substitutions, third most frequent in crib speech, were the least frequent type of practice in social-context speech. Breakdowns were the fourth most frequent type of practice in crib speech but the second most frequent type of practice in social-context speech.

Child F

Once again, breakdowns were more common when another person provided the model than when the child provided the model. Each of the other types of practice was more common when Child F produced the model utterance than when another person did so (Table 4-36). There was also an interaction between type of model and practice type (Table 4-37). Breakdowns, the least frequent type of practice in self-model practice, were the second most frequent type of practice when another person provided the original utterance. Completions, the third most frequent type of practice when the child produced the model, were the least frequent type of model when another person provided the model.

Each type of practice was least likely to be produced in asocial speech insofar as practice based on self-models was concerned (Table 4-38). Buildups, breakdowns,

Table 4-36. Comparison of Each Practice Type When Produced Following a Self-Model or an Other-Model (Child F)

Practice Type	Most Common with Self-Model or Other-Model	Absolute Numbers (self-other)
Buildups	Self	210-34
Breakdowns	Other	101-154
Completions	Self	146-17
Exact reproductions	Self	510-189
Substitutions	Self	138-31

Table 4-37. Rank Order of Absolute Frequencies (from most to least frequent) of Each Practice Type When the Model Was Produced by the Self or by Another (Child F)

Model	
Self	Other
Exact reproductions	Exact reproductions
Buildups	Breakdowns
Completions	Buildups
Substitutions	Substitutions
Breakdowns	Completions

Table 4-38. Rank Order of Each Practice Type in Each of the Three Self-Model Situations (Child F)

Practice Type	Most Frequent[a]	Next Most Frequent[a]	Least Frequent[a]
Buildups	Crib (150)	Social (47)	Asocial (13)
Breakdowns	Crib (89)	Social (10)	Asocial (2)
Completions	Crib (106)	Social (35)	Asocial (5)
Exact reproductions	Social (208)	Crib (185)	Asocial (117)
Substitutions	Crib (90)	Social (31)	Asocial (17)

[a]Numbers in parentheses indicate the number of instances of each practice type in each of the three situations.

completions, and substitutions were more likely to be produced in crib speech than in social speech or asocial speech. Exact reproductions were more common in social speech than in crib speech or asocial speech.

Buildups and completions were more common in crib speech than in social-context speech (combining the three types of social-context speech), whereas breakdowns, exact reproductions, and substitutions were more common in social-context speech than in crib speech (Table 4-39). There was an interaction between

Table 4-39. Comparison of Each Type of Practice in Crib Speech and Social-Context Speech (Child F)

Practice Type	Most Common in Crib or Social-Context	Absolute Numbers (crib-social)
Buildups	Crib	150–94
Breakdowns	Social	89–166
Completions	Crib	106–57
Exact reproductions	Social	185–514
Substitutions	Social	185–356

Table 4-40. Rank Order of Absolute Frequency (from most to least frequent) of Each Type of Practice in Crib Speech and in Social-Context Speech (Child F)

Speech Type	
Crib	Social-Context
Exact reproductions	Exact reproductions
Buildups	Breakdowns
Completions	Buildups
Substitutions	Substitutions
Breakdowns	Completions

speech type and type of practice (Table 4-40). Breakdowns, the least common type of practice in crib speech, were the second most common type of practice in social-context speech. Completions, the third most common type of practice in crib speech, were the least common type of practice in social-context speech.

Child G

Breakdowns were more common when another person produced the model utterance than when Child G produced the model, with the opposite pattern holding for the other four types of practice (Table 4-41). There was once again an interaction between type of model and type of practice (Table 4-42). Buildups, the second most frequent type of practice based on self-models, were the least frequent type of practice when another produced the model utterance. Breakdowns, the third most frequent type of practice based on self-models, were the most frequent type of practice based on other-models. Completions, the least frequent type of practice for self-models, were the third most frequent type of practice when another person produced the model.

Buildups, breakdowns, and exact reproductions were more frequent in crib speech than in either other type of self-model context (Table 4-43). Completions and substitutions were more common in asocial speech than in crib speech or social speech. For Child G, practice seemed most likely to occur when there was no com-

Table 4-41. Comparison of Each Practice Type When Produced Following a Self-Model or an Other-Model (Child G)

Practice Type	Most Common with Self-Model or Other-Model	Absolute Numbers (self-other)
Buildups	Self	30-2
Breakdowns	Other	30-309
Completions	Self	5-3
Exact reproductions	Self	212-127
Substitutions	Self	24-3

Table 4-42. Rank Order of Absolute Frequencies (from most to least frequent) of Each Practice Type When the Model Was Produced by the Self or by Another (Child G)

Model	
Self	Other
Exact reproductions	Breakdowns
Buildups	Exact reproductions
Breakdowns	Completions
Substitutions	Substitutions
Completions	Buildups

Table 4-43. Rank Order of Each Practice Type in Each of the Three Self-Model Situations (Child G)

Practice Type	Most Frequent[a]	Next Most Frequent[a]	Least Frequent[a]
Buildups	Crib (18)	Social (8)	Asocial (4)
Breakdowns	Crib (16)	Asocial (8)	Social (6)
Completions	Asocial (3)	Crib/social (1 each)	
Exact reproductions	Crib (96)	Social (88)	Asocial (28)
Substitutions	Asocial (12)	Social (9)	Crib (3)

[a]Numbers in parentheses indicate the number of instances of each practice type in each of the three situations.

municative intent (crib speech or asocial speech). However, there was not a perfect correspondence between communicative intent and linguistic practice. Buildups and exact repetitions were more common in social speech than in asocial speech. Substitutions were more common in social speech than in crib speech. One instance of a completion was produced in both crib speech and in social speech. Child G's tendency, then, was just that—a tendency rather than an absolute predisposition.

Buildups were more common in crib speech than in social-context speech

Table 4-44. Comparison of Each Type of Practice in Crib Speech and Social-Context Speech (Child G)

Practice Type	Most Common in Crib or Social-Context	Absolute Numbers (crib-social)
Buildups	Crib	18-14
Breakdowns	Social	16-323
Completions	Social	1-5
Exact reproductions	Social	96-243
Substitutions	Social	3-24

Table 4-45. Rank Order of Absolute Frequency (from most to least frequent) of Each Type of Practice in Crib Speech and in Social-Context Speech (Child G)

Speech Type	
Crib	Social-Context
Exact reproductions	Breakdowns
Buildups	Exact reproductions
Breakdowns	Substitutions
Substitutions	Buildups
Completions	Completions

(combining the three types of social-context speech), the other four types of practice exhibiting the opposite pattern (Table 4-44). There was once again an interaction between type of speech and type of practice (Table 4-45). Buildups were the second most frequent type of practice in crib speech but the fourth most frequent type of practice in social-context speech. Breakdowns, the third most frequent type of practice in crib speech, were the most common type of practice in social-context speech.

Child H

Buildups, completions, and exact reproductions were more common when the model utterance was produced by Child H than when the model was produced by another. Breakdowns and substitutions were more common when another person produced the model than when Child H produced the model (Table 4-46). The interaction between type of model and type of practice is shown in Table 4-47. Buildups and breakdowns were second and fourth most frequent, respectively, in practice based on self-models, but fourth and second, respectively, in terms of absolute frequency for practice based on other-models. Completions and substitutions were the third and fifth most frequent types of practice, respectively, based on self-models, but the fifth and third most frequent types of practice, respectively,

Table 4-46. Comparison of Each Practice Type When Produced Following a Self-Model or an Other-Model (Child H)

Practice Type	Most Common with Self-Model or Other-Model	Absolute Numbers (self-other)
Buildups	Self	291-58
Breakdowns	Other	199-287
Completions	Self	246-3
Exact reproductions	Self	1216-397
Substitutions	Other	136-175

Table 4-47. Rank Order of Absolute Frequencies (from most to least frequent) of Each Practice Type When the Model Was Produced by the Self or by Another (Child H)

Model	
Self	Other
Exact reproductions	Exact reproductions
Buildups	Breakdowns
Completions	Substitutions
Breakdowns	Buildups
Substitutions	Completions

based on other-models. Once again, the rank order of exact reproductions was unaffected by the type of model.

For practice based on self-models, buildups, breakdowns, completions and substitutions were most frequent in crib speech. Exact repetitions were more frequent in social speech than in crib speech or asocial speech. Each type of practice was second most frequently produced in asocial speech. This data is summarized in Table 4-48. Child H was most likely to engage in linguistic practice in noncommunicative settings.

Table 4-48. Rank Order of Each Practice Type in Each of the Three Self-Model Situations (Child H)

Practice Type	Most Frequent[a]	Next Most Frequent[a]	Least Frequent[a]
Buildups	Crib (217)	Asocial (63)	Social (11)
Breakdowns	Crib (143)	Asocial (47)	Social (9)
Completions	Crib (196)	Asocial (402)	Social (18)
Exact reproductions	Social (455)	Asocial (402)	Crib (359)
Substitutions	Crib (97)	Asocial (30)	Social (9)

[a]Numbers in parentheses indicate the number of instances of each practice type in each of the three situations.

Table 4-49. Comparison of Each Type of Practice in Crib Speech and Social-Context Speech (Child H)

Practice Type	Most Common in Crib or Social-Context	Absolute Numbers (crib-social)
Buildups	Crib	217-132
Breakdowns	Social	143-343
Completions	Crib	196-53
Exact reproductions	Social	359-1254
Substitutions	Social	97-214

Table 4-50. Rank Order of Absolute Frequency (from most to least frequent) of Each Type of Practice in Crib Speech and in Social-Context Speech (Child H)

Speech Type	
Crib	Social-Context
Exact reproductions	Exact reproductions
Buildups	Breakdowns
Completions	Substitutions
Breakdowns	Buildups
Substitutions	Completions

Buildups and completions were more common in crib speech than in social-context speech (Table 4-49). The opposite pattern held for breakdowns, completions, and substitutions. The interaction of speech type and practice type is shown in Table 4-50. Buildups and breakdowns were the second and fourth most frequent practice types, respectively, in crib speech, but the fourth and second most frequent practice types, respectively, in social-context speech. Completions and substitutions were the third and fifth most frequent types of practice, respectively, in crib speech, but the fifth and third most frequent types of practice, respectively, in social-context speech.

Child I

Breakdowns were more common when the practice was based on another's model utterance than when it was based on Child I's model utterance (Table 4-51). The remaining four types of practice were more common when Child I produced the model than when an adult produced the model. There was also an interaction between type of model and type of practice (Table 4-52). Breakdowns were the least common type of practice when Child I produced the model, but the second most frequent type of practice when an adult produced the model. Buildups were the third most common type of practice for self-models, but the least frequent type of practice when the model was produced by another.

Table 4-51. Comparison of Each Practice Type When Produced Following a Self-Model or an Other-Model (Child I)

Practice Type	Most Common with Self-Model or Other-Model	Absolute Numbers (self-other)
Buildups	Self	92-1
Breakdowns	Other	11-91
Completions	Self	37-10
Exact reproductions	Self	279-119
Substitutions	Self	102-14

Table 4-52. Rank Order of Absolute Frequencies (from most to least frequent) of Each
Practice Type When the Model Was Produced
by the Self or by Another (Child I)

Model	
Self	Other
Exact reproductions	Exact reproductions
Substitutions	Breakdowns
Buildups	Substitutions
Completions	Completions
Breakdowns	Buildups

Table 4-53. Rank Order of Each Practice Type in Each of the Three Self-Model
Situations (Child I)

Practice Type	Most Frequent[a]	Next Most Frequent[a]	Least Frequent[a]
Buildups	Asocial (39)	Crib (32)	Social (21)
Breakdowns	Crib (6)	Asocial (3)	Social (2)
Completions	Crib/asocial (13 each)		Social (11)
Exact reproductions	Crib (138)	Social (83)	Asocial (58)
Substitutions	Crib (77)	Asocial (17)	Asocial (8)

[a]Numbers in parentheses indicate the number of instances of each practice type in each of the
three situations.

Breakdowns, exact repetitions, and substitutions were more frequently produced in crib speech than in either other type of self-model situation (Table 4-53).
Completions were produced with the same frequency in crib speech and in asocial
speech, and least often in social speech. Buildups were more frequent in asocial
speech than in crib speech or social speech. With the exception of exact reproductions, each type of practice was least frequent in social speech. This suggests that
Child I was most likely to produce practice when the utterance had no communi-

Table 4-54. Comparison of Each Type of Practice in Crib Speech
and Social-Context Speech (Child I)

Practice Type	Most Common in Crib or Social-Context	Absolute Numbers (crib-social)
Buildups	Social	32-61
Breakdowns	Social	6-96
Completions	Social	13-34
Exact reproductions	Social	138-260
Substitutions	Crib	77-39

Table 4-55. Rank Order of Absolute Frequency (from most to least frequent) of Each Type of Practice in Crib Speech and in Social-Context Speech (Child I)

Speech Type	
Crib	Social-Context
Exact reproductions	Exact reproductions
Substitutions	Breakdowns
Buildups	Buildups
Completions	Substitutions
Breakdowns	Completions

cative intent, at least insofar as practice based on self-models is concerned. For Child I, this does not mean that crib speech was the primary context in which linguistic practice occurred, only that practice was more likely to occur in noncommunicative contexts when the practice was based on self-models. Comparing practice in crib speech with practice in social-context speech (combining the three types of social-context speech) revealed a different pattern. Substitutions were more common in crib speech than in social-context speech, with the remaining four types of practice exhibiting the opposite pattern (Table 4-54). The interaction of speech type and practice type is shown in Table 4-55. Breakdowns were the least frequent type of practice in crib speech, but the second most frequent type of practice in social-context speech. Substitutions were the second most frequent type of practice in crib speech, but the fourth most frequent type of practice in social-context speech.

Child J

Breakdowns were more frequently produced when an adult provided the model than when Child J provided the model. The remaining four types of practice were more common when the practice was based on self-models than when the practice was based on other-models (Table 4-56). The interaction of type of model and type of practice is shown in Table 4-57. Buildups, the second most common type of

Table 4-56. Comparison of Each Practice Type When Produced Following a Self-Model or an Other-Model (Child J)

Practice Type	Most Common with Self-Model or Other-Model	Absolute Numbers (self-other)
Buildups	Self	69-4
Breakdowns	Other	54-85
Completions	Self	3-1
Exact reproductions	Self	869-35
Substitutions	Self	49-13

Table 4-57. Rank Order of Absolute Frequencies (from most to least frequent) of Each
Practice Type When the Model Was Produced
by the Self or by Another (Child J)

Model	
Self	Other
Exact reproductions	Breakdowns
Buildups	Exact reproductions
Breakdowns	Substitutions
Substitutions	Buildups
Completions	Completions

practice when Child J provided the model, were the fourth most frequent type of
practice when an adult provided the model. Breakdowns, the third most frequent
type of practice when Child J provided the model, were the most frequent practice
type when an adult provided the model.

In regard to practice based on model utterances produced by the child, buildups,

Table 4-58. Rank Order of Each Practice Type in Each of the Three Self-Model
Situations (Child J)

Practice Type	Most Frequent[a]	Next Most Frequent[a]	Least Frequent[a]
Buildups	Social (39)	Crib (26)	Asocial (4)
Breakdowns	Social (30)	Crib (22)	Asocial (2)
Completions	Social (3)	Crib/asocial (0 each)	
Exact reproductions	Crib (440)	Social (331)	Asocial (98)
Substitutions	Crib (25)	Social (21)	Asocial (3)

[a]Numbers in parentheses indicate the number of instances of each practice type in each of the
three situations.

Table 4-59. Rank Order of Absolute Fre-
quency (from most to least frequent) of Each
Type of Practice in Crib Speech and in Social-
Context Speech (Child J)

Speech Type	
Crib	Social-Context
Exact reproductions	Exact reproductions
Buildups	Breakdowns
Substitutions	Buildups
Breakdowns	Substitutions
Completions	Completions

Table 4-60. Comparison of Each Type of Practice in Crib Speech and Social-Context Speech (Child J)

Practice Type	Most Common in Crib or Social-Context	Absolute Numbers (crib-social)
Buildups	Social	26-47
Breakdowns	Social	22-117
Completions	Social	0-4
Exact reproductions	Social	440-464
Substitutions	Social	25-37

breakdowns, and completions were more common in social speech than in crib speech or asocial speech (Table 4-58). Exact reproductions and substitutions were more common in crib speech than in social speech or asocial speech. Child J consistently produced the least amount of self-model practice in asocial speech (see Table 4-59).

Each type of practice was more common in social-context speech (combining the three types of social-context speech) than in crib speech (Table 4-60). There was once again an interaction of type of practice and type of speech. Breakdowns were the fourth most frequent type of practice in crib speech but the second most common type in social-context speech.

Child K

Each type of practice was more likely to occur when the model was produced by Child K rather than by an adult (Table 4-61). The interaction of type of model and type of practice is shown in Table 4-62. Breakdowns were the least frequent type of practice when the utterance was based on Child K's model, but the second most frequent type of practice when another person provided the model. Buildups, breakdowns, completions, and substitutions were most likely to occur in crib speech, a situation in which the model was produced by Child K (Table 4-63). Exact reproductions were more likely to occur in social speech than in crib speech or asocial speech. Four of the five types of practice (the exception being breakdowns) were

Table 4-61. Comparison of Each Practice Type When Produced Following a Self-Model or an Other-Model (Child K)

Practice Type	Most Common with Self-Model or Other-Model	Absolute Numbers (self-other)
Buildups	Self	272-45
Breakdowns	Self	166-160
Completions	Self	219-36
Exact reproductions	Self	552-395
Substitutions	Self	201-34

Table 4-62. Rank Order of Absolute Frequencies (from most to least frequent) of Each Practice Type When the Model Was Produced by the Self or by Another (Child K)

Model	
Self	Other
Exact reproductions	Exact reproductions
Buildups	Breakdowns
Completions	Buildups
Substitutions	Completions
Breakdowns	Substitutions

Table 4-63. Rank Order of Each Practice Type in Each of the Three Self-Model Situations (Child K)

Practice Type	Most Frequent[a]	Next Most Frequent[a]	Least Frequent[a]
Buildups	Crib (221)	Social (33)	Asocial (18)
Breakdowns	Crib (135)	Asocial (25)	Social (6)
Completions	Crib (97)	Social (77)	Asocial (45)
Exact reproductions	Social (273)	Crib (186)	Asocial (93)
Substitutions	Crib (150)	Social (28)	Asocial (23)

[a]Numbers in parentheses indicate the number of instances of each practice type in each of the three situations.

least likely to occur in asocial speech. For Child K, crib speech appeared to be a particularly salient context in which language practice might occur (at least insofar as practice based on self-models was concerned).

Buildups and substitutions were more likely to occur in crib speech than in social-context speech (combining the three types of social-context speech). Breakdowns, completions, and exact reproductions were more frequent in social-context speech than in crib speech. These patterns are summarized in Table 4-64. The inter-

Table 4-64. Comparison of Each Type of Practice in Crib Speech and Social-Context Speech (Child K)

Practice Type	Most Common in Crib or Social-Context	Absolute Numbers (crib-social)
Buildups	Crib	221-96
Breakdowns	Social	135-191
Completions	Social	97-158
Exact reproductions	Social	186-761
Substitutions	Crib	150-85

Table 4-65. Rank Order of Absolute Frequency (from most to least frequent) of Each Type of Practice in Crib Speech and in Social-Context Speech (Child K)

Speech Type	
Crib	Social-Context
Buildups	Exact reproductions
Exact reproductions	Breakdowns
Substitutions	Completions
Breakdowns	Buildups
Completions	Substitutions

action of speech type and practice type is shown in Table 4-65. Buildups, the most common type of practice in crib speech, were the fourth most common type of practice in social-context speech. Substitutions and completions, the third and fifth most frequent types of practice, respectively, in crib speech, were the fifth and third most frequent types of practice, respectively, in social-context speech. Breakdowns were the fourth most common type of practice in crib speech but the second most common type of practice in social-context speech.

Child L

Breakdowns were once again the only type of practice more likely to occur following a model produced by an adult rather than one produced by a child. The remaining four types of practice exhibited the opposite pattern (Table 4-66). The interaction between type of model and type of practice is shown in Table 4-67. Substitutions were the second most frequent type of practice when Child L produced the model, but the fourth most frequent type of practice when another person produced the model. Breakdowns were the least frequent type of practice when Child L produced the model, but the second most frequent type of practice when another person produced the model.

For practice based on self-models, buildups, breakdowns, completions, and substitutions were more common in crib speech than in social speech or asocial speech.

Table 4-66. Comparison of Each Practice Type When Produced Following a Self-Model or an Other-Model (Child L)

Practice Type	Most Common with Self-Model or Other-Model	Absolute Numbers (self-other)
Buildups	Self	59-14
Breakdowns	Other	24-105
Completions	Self	59-10
Exact reproductions	Self	210-151
Substitutions	Self	70-11

Table 4-67. Rank Order of Absolute Frequencies (from most to least frequent) of Each Practice Type When the Model Was Produced by the Self or by Another (Child L)

Model	
Self	Other
Exact reproductions	Exact reproductions
Substitutions	Breakdowns
Buildups	Buildups
Completions tie	Substitutions
Breakdowns	Completions

Exact reproductions were more common in asocial speech than in crib speech or social speech. These data are summarized in Table 4-68. For practice based on self-models, Child L was more likely to produce each type of practice in noncommunicative contexts than in communicative contexts.

Buildups and substitutions were more common in crib speech than in social-context speech (Table 4-69). Breakdowns, completions, and exact reproductions were more common in social-context speech than in crib speech. There was also an

Table 4-68. Rank Order of Each Practice Type in Each of the Three Self-Model Situations (Child L)

Practice Type	Most Frequent[a]	Next Most Frequent[a]	Least Frequent[a]
Buildups	Crib (46)	Social (8)	Asocial (5)
Breakdowns	Crib (19)	Asocial (3)	Social (2)
Completions	Crib (29)	Social/asocial (15 each)	
Exact reproductions	Asocial (118)	Crib (65)	Social (27)
Substitutions	Crib (48)	Social (14)	Asocial (8)

[a]Numbers in parentheses indicate the number of instances of each practice type in each of the three situations.

Table 4-69. Comparison of Each Type of Practice in Crib Speech and Social-Context Speech (Child L)

Practice Type	Most Common in Crib or Social-Context	Absolute Numbers (crib-social)
Buildups	Crib	46-27
Breakdowns	Social	19-110
Completions	Social	29-40
Exact reproductions	Social	65-296
Substitutions	Crib	48-33

Table 4-70. Rank Order of Absolute Frequency (from most to least frequent) of Each Type of Practice in Crib Speech and in Social-Context Speech (Child L)

Speech Type	
Crib	Social-Context
Exact reproductions	Exact reproductions
Substitutions	Breakdowns
Buildups	Completions
Completions	Substitutions
Breakdowns	Buildups

interaction between type of speech and type of practice (Table 4-70). Substitutions were the second most frequent type of practice in crib speech but the fourth most frequent type of practice in social-context speech. Buildups were the third most frequent type of practice in crib speech but the least frequent type of practice in social-context speech. Breakdowns, the least frequent type of practice in crib speech, were the second most frequent type of practice in social-context speech.

Child M

As usual, breakdowns were the only type of practice to occur more often when an adult produced the model utterance than when the child produced the model utterance (Table 4-71). The interaction of type of model and type of practice is shown in Table 4-72. Buildups were the most frequent type of practice when Child M produced the model but the fourth least frequent type of practice when another produced the model. Breakdowns, the third most frequent type of practice based on self-models, were the most frequent type of practice based on other-models.

For practice based on self-models, buildups, breakdowns, and substitutions were more frequent in crib speech than in social speech or asocial speech. Completions and exact reproductions were more common in social speech than in crib speech or asocial speech. Each type of practice was least frequent in asocial speech (there were eight instances of substitutions in both social speech and in asocial speech, so

Table 4-71. Comparison of Each Practice Type When Produced Following a Self-Model or an Other-Model (Child M)

Practice Type	Most Common with Self-Model or Other-Model	Absolute Numbers (self-other)
Buildups	Self	174–5
Breakdowns	Other	84–124
Completions	Self	51–4
Exact reproductions	Self	118–35
Substitutions	Self	67–10

Table 4-72. Rank Order of Absolute Frequencies (from most to least frequent) of Each Practice Type When the Model Was Produced by the Self or by Another (Child M)

Model	
Self	Other
Buildups	Breakdowns
Exact reproductions	Exact reproductions
Breakdowns	Substitutions
Substitutions	Buildups
Completions	Completions

in this case social speech and asocial speech yielded equal numbers of practice tokens). These data are summarized in Table 4-73.

Buildups and substitutions were more frequent in crib speech than in social-context speech (Table 4-74). Breakdowns, completions, and exact reproductions were more common in social-context speech than in crib speech. The interaction of speech type and practice type is shown in Table 4-75. The most notable interaction concerned buildups. They were the most frequent type of practice in crib speech, but the third most common type of practice in social-context speech.

Table 4-73. Rank Order of Each Practice Type in Each of the Three Self-Model Situations (Child M)

Practice Type	Most Frequent[a]	Next Most Frequent[a]	Least Frequent[a]
Buildups	Crib (128)	Social (39)	Asocial (7)
Breakdowns	Crib (65)	Asocial (11)	Social (8)
Completions	Social (30)	Crib (16)	Asocial (5)
Exact reproductions	Social (53)	Crib (52)	Asocial (13)
Substitutions	Crib (51)	Social/asocial (8 each)	

[a]Numbers in parentheses indicate the number of instances of each practice type in each of the three situations.

Table 4-74. Comparison of Each Type of Practice in Crib Speech and Social-Context Speech (Child M)

Practice Type	Most Common in Crib or Social-Context	Absolute Numbers (crib-social)
Buildups	Crib	128-51
Breakdowns	Social	65-143
Completions	Social	16-39
Exact reproductions	Social	52-101
Substitutions	Crib	51-26

Table 4-75. Rank Order of Absolute Frequency (from most to least frequent) of Each Type of Practice in Crib Speech and in Social-Context Speech (Child M)

Speech Type	
Crib	Social-Context
Buildups	Breakdowns
Breakdowns	Exact reproductions
Exact reproductions	Buildups
Substitutions	Completions
Completions	Substitutions

Child N

Each type of practice was more frequent when the model was produced by Child N rather than by an adult (Table 4-76). The interaction of type of model and type of practice is shown in Table 4-77. The most significant difference concerned breakdowns. Breakdowns were the third most frequent type of practice based on self-models, but the most frequent type of practice based on other-models.

Each type of practice was more common in crib speech than in either other type

Table 4-76. Comparison of Each Practice Type When Produced Following a Self-Model or an Other-Model (Child N)

Practice Type	Most Common with Self-Model or Other-Model	Absolute Numbers (self-other)
Buildups	Self	421-39
Breakdowns	Self	360-265
Completions	Self	183-0
Exact reproductions	Self	699-249
Substitutions	Self	92-5

Table 4-77. Rank Order of Absolute Frequencies (from most to least frequent) of Each Practice Type When the Model Was Produced by the Self or by Another (Child N)

Model	
Self	Other
Exact reproductions	Breakdowns
Buildups	Exact reproductions
Breakdowns	Buildups
Completions	Substitutions
Substitutions	Completions

Table 4-78. Rank Order of Each Practice Type in Each of the Three Self-Model Situations (Child N)

Practice Type	Most Frequent[a]	Next Most Frequent[a]	Least Frequent[a]
Buildups	Crib (198)	Social (180)	Asocial (43)
Breakdowns	Crib (172)	Asocial (113)	Social (75)
Completions	Crib (101)	Social (67)	Asocial (15)
Exact reproductions	Crib (286)	Social (249)	Asocial (164)
Substitutions	Crib (40)	Social (39)	Asocial (13)

[a]Numbers in parentheses indicate the number of instances of each practice type in each of the three situations.

Table 4-79. Comparison of Each Type of Practice in Crib Speech and Social-Context Speech (Child N)

Practice Type	Most Common in Crib or Social-Context	Absolute Numbers (crib-social)
Buildups	Social	198-262
Breakdowns	Social	172-453
Completions	Crib	101-82
Exact reproductions	Social	286-662
Substitutions	Social	40-57

of practice based on self-models (Table 4-78). With the exception of breakdowns, each type of practice was least frequent in asocial speech. For Child N, crib speech was the more optimal noncommunicative speech setting insofar as practice based on self-models was concerned. Combining the three types of social-context speech, completions were more frequent in crib speech than in social-context speech (Table 4-79). The remaining types of practice were more common in social-context speech than in crib speech. The interaction of speech type and practice type is

Table 4-80. Rank Order of Absolute Frequency (from most to least frequent) of Each Type of Practice in Crib Speech and in Social-Context Speech (Child N)

Speech Type	
Crib	Social-Context
Exact reproductions	Exact reproductions
Buildups	Breakdowns
Breakdowns	Buildups
Completions	Completions
Substitutions	Substitutions

shown in Table 4-80. This table reveals that there were not many differences in the rank orders of practice types in two speech sampling situations.

Summary

The preceding analyses of the interaction of practice type, model type, and speech type reveal that, in spite of the many individual differences, there are certain general developmental patterns that are fairly consistent across children. Before going on to a consideration of the developmental patterns revealed by each child, I will summarize the general patterns found in the analyses just given. However, the reader is urged to remember that these patterns, unless otherwise noted, are general tendencies rather than absolute predispositions.

1. Each child was more likely to produce buildups, completions, and exact reproductions following a self-produced model rather than an other-produced model utterance. Thirteen of the children were more likely to produce substitutions following a self-model rather than a model produced by an adult. The remaining child (H) exhibited the opposite pattern for substitutions. Eleven of the children were more likely to produce breakdowns following a model produced by another rather than a self-model. The remaining three children (A, K, and N) exhibited the opposite pattern.

2. The interaction of type of model and type of practice also yielded certain consistent patterns. A comparison of the rank orders of practice types following self-models and following other-models revealed that breakdowns were relatively more frequent following other-models rather than self-models. This was true for each child. For seven of the children (D, E, G, H, I, J, and M), buildups were relatively more frequent following self-models rather than other-models. For five of the children (A, B, F, G, and H), completions were relatively more frequent following self-models rather than other-models.

3. Comparing the frequency of each type of practice in the three self-model situations (crib speech, social speech, and asocial speech) demonstrated the importance of crib speech as a self-model situation. Buildups were most likely to occur in crib speech, next most likely to occur in social speech, and least likely to occur in asocial speech. Breakdowns were most likely to occur in crib speech, next most likely to occur in asocial speech, and least likely to occur in social speech. Completions were most likely to occur in either crib speech or social speech, and least likely to occur in asocial speech. Exact reproductions were most likely to occur in crib speech, next most likely to occur in social speech, and least likely to occur in asocial speech. Substitutions were most likely to occur in crib speech, next most likely to occur in asocial speech, and least likely to occur in social speech.

4. Each child was more likely to produce breakdowns and exact reproductions in social-context speech than in crib speech. Ten of the children were more likely to produce completions in social-context speech than in crib speech. The remaining four children (B, F, H, and N) exhibited the opposite pattern. Eight children were more likely to produce substitutions in social-context speech than in crib speech, the remaining six children (A, B, I, K, L, and M) exhibiting the opposite pattern. Eight children were more likely to produce buildups in crib speech than in social-

context speech, the remaining six children (C, D, E, I, J, and N) exhibiting the opposite pattern.

5. The rank orders of practice types in crib speech and in social-context speech revealed an interaction of speech type and practice type. Breakdowns were relatively more frequent in social-context speech than in crib speech for 12 of the children. Buildups were relatively more frequent in crib speech than in social-context speech for seven of the children.

These analyses have demonstrated that the type of model (produced by the child or by another person) and the type of speech setting (crib or social-context) influence the relative frequency of each type of practice. However, these analyses, although concerned with the practice of individual children, did not take into consideration possible developmental patterns that might exist. The following analyses focus on such developmental patterns, that is, on changes over time for each child. The discussion of individual developmental patterns will focus on three analyses: (a) the relative frequency of each type of practice within each speech sample, determined by dividing the number of instances of a practice type (e.g., buildups) in a speech sample by the total number of practice instances (combining the five types of practice) in that speech sample. These comparisons of the relative frequencies of each practice type *within* a speech sample for all speech samples by each child make it possible to determine if such relative frequencies for a practice type vary with age and if the relative frequencies for each practice type are different for crib speech and social-context speech. (b) The second analysis concerns the relative frequency of each type of practice *across* speech samples for each child, determined by dividing the number of instances of a practice type (e.g., buildups) in a speech sample by the total number of instances of that practice type in all of the samples of that speech type (crib speech or social-context speech). This analysis makes possible the determination of developmental tendencies in the use of each type of practice (e.g., are buildups equally distributed across samples or concentrated at particular developmental periods?) as well as making possible a comparison of the developmental patterns in crib speech and in social-context speech. This analysis of relative frequency of practice across samples, coupled with the analysis of relative frequency of practice within samples, should clarify the developmental patterns inherent in the practice of language skills. (c) The final type of analysis involves the comparison of the two types of relative frequencies with MLU. The intent of this analysis is to compare the peaks and valleys of each type of relative frequency with those of MLU.

Analyses of Developmental Patterns: Buildups

Within-Sample Comparisons

The within-sample comparisons for buildups are shown in Figures 4-1 through 4-14. Buildups consistently (i.e., across speech samples) comprised a greater proportion of practice in crib speech than in social-context speech for seven of the children (A, B, F, H, K, L, and M). Buildups also comprised a larger proportion of crib-

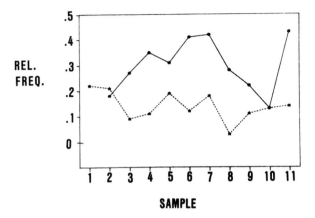

Figure 4-1. Within-sample comparisons of the relative frequency of buildups in the crib speech and social-context speech of Child A. The solid line denotes crib speech. The dashed line denotes social-context speech.

speech practice than social-context-speech practice for Child C (see Figure 4-3), consistently so in samples 8 through 15. Prior to sample 8, there was no appreciable difference between the relative frequency of buildups in crib speech and in social-context speech. Following sample 15, buildups occasionally constituted a greater proportion of practice in crib speech than in social-context speech. However, there was more variability in these later crib-speech samples, resulting in many peaks and valleys. Child G's early speech samples revealed no substantial difference between proportion of practice in crib speech and in social-context speech (see Figure 4-7). When there were substantial differences between the relative frequencies of buildups in the two speech types for Child G, buildups were more frequent

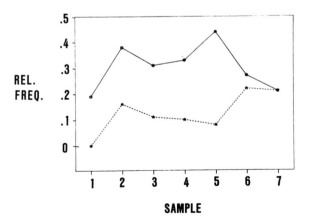

Figure 4-2. Within-sample comparisons of the relative frequency of buildups in the crib speech and social-context speech of Child B. The solid line denotes crib speech. The dashed line denotes social-context speech.

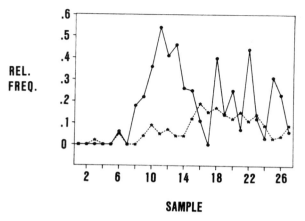

Figure 4-3. Within-sample comparisons of the relative frequency of buildups in the crib speech and social-context speech of Child C. The solid line denotes crib speech. The dashed line denotes social-context speech.

in crib speech than in social context speech (samples 6, 7, 11, 12, 13). Child N's speech samples revealed considerable variability in regard to the relative frequency of buildups in crib speech and in social-context speech (see Figure 4-14). In the early speech samples of Child N, buildups tended to constitute a larger proportion of practice in crib speech than in social-context speech. There was considerably more variability in the later speech samples. The remaining four children (D, E, I, J) exhibited no difference in the relative frequency of buildups in crib speech and in social-context speech or greater relative frequency in social-context speech than in crib speech.

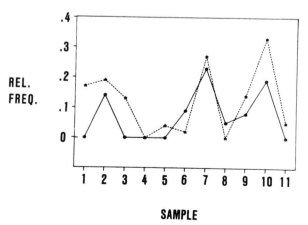

Figure 4-4. Within-sample comparisons of the relative frequency of buildups in the crib speech and social-context speech of Child D. The solid line denotes crib speech. The dashed line denotes social-context speech.

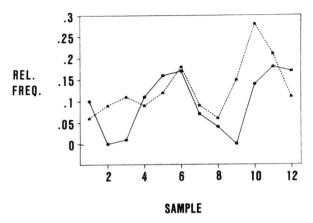

Figure 4-5. Within-sample comparisons of the relative frequency of buildups in the crib speech and social-context speech of Child E. The solid line denotes crib speech. The dashed line denotes social-context speech.

For three children (C, D, L), buildups constituted a larger proportion of linguistic practice in the early crib-speech samples than in the later crib-speech samples, the opposite pattern holding for social-context speech. This finding supports the notion that crib speech may serve as a "trying ground" for language skills and language-learning strategies. Although the remaining 11 children did not conform to this pattern, no child exhibited the opposite pattern.

The relative frequency of buildups was more variable across samples in crib speech than in social-context speech for nine of the children (A, B, C, F, G, H, K, L, and N). There was more variability in social-context speech than in crib speech

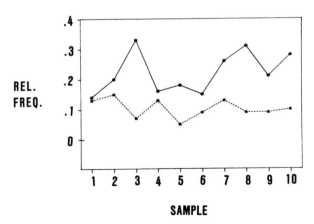

Figure 4-6. Within-sample comparisons of the relative frequency of buildups in the crib speech and social-context speech of Child F. The solid line denotes crib speech. The dashed line denotes social-context speech.

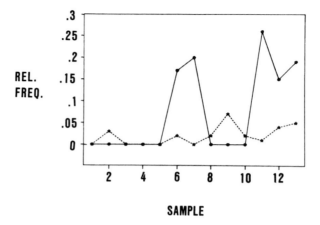

SAMPLE

Figure 4-7. Within-sample comparisons of the relative frequency of buildups in the crib speech and social-context speech of Child G. The solid line denotes crib speech. The dashed line denotes social-context speech.

(although marginally so) for Child I and Child M (see Figures 4-9 and 4-14). There was no substantial difference in variability in crib speech and in social-context speech for the remaining three children (D, E, and F; see Figures 4-4 through 4-6).

Six of the children (A, B, F, H, K, and L) exhibited the inverse relation between peaks and valleys for buildups in crib speech and in social-context speech that was frequently observed for MLU (see Chapter 3). For these children, an increase in the relative frequency of buildups in crib speech tended to correspond with a decrease in the relative frequency of buildups in social-context speech, and vice versa. For two of the children (D and E), the developmental patterns revealed for the relative frequency of buildups is quite similar in crib speech and in social-context speech.

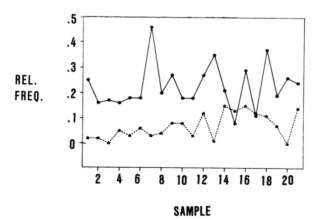

SAMPLE

Figure 4-8. Within-sample comparisons of the relative frequency of buildups in the crib speech and social-context speech of Child H. The solid line denotes crib speech. The dashed line denotes social-context speech.

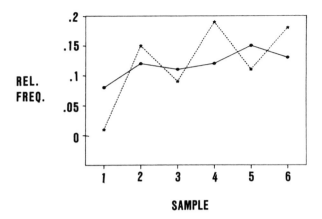

Figure 4-9. Within-sample comparisons of the relative frequency of buildups in the crib speech and social-context speech of Child I. The solid line denotes crib speech. The dashed line denotes social-context speech.

The developmental patterns evidenced by four other children (C, J, M, and N) contain occasional inverse relations among peaks and valleys, but contain many similar patterns in regard to increases and decreases in relative frequency. There was no apparent relation among the relative frequency of buildups in crib speech and in social-context speech for the remaining two children (G and I).

The final analysis compared the MLUs and the relative frequency of buildups of each child. This analysis revealed no relation between relative frequency of buildups and MLU for social-context speech for any child, but parallel developmental patterns for MLU and relative frequency of buildups in crib speech for children A, D, and G. This relation was also found in the speech of Child B (except for the last

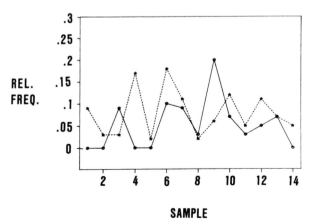

Figure 4-10. Within-sample comparisons of the relative frequency of buildups in the crib speech and social-context speech of Child J. The solid line denotes crib speech. The dashed line denotes social-context speech.

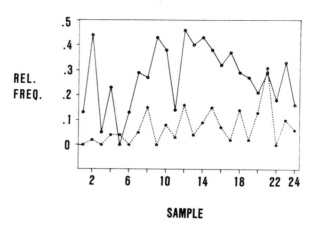

Figure 4-11. Within-sample comparisons of the relative frequency of buildups in the crib speech and social-context speech of Child K. The solid line denotes crib speech. The dashed line denotes social-context speech.

sample), Child F (for the first samples), and children C and L (for the observed peaks). For these children, then, the fluctuation in relative frequency of buildups in crib speech from week to week paralleled the fluctuation of crib speech MLU from week to week.

There is another type of developmental relation to be considered. This is one in which a peak in the relative frequency of buildups in one crib-speech sample is followed by a substantial increase in MLU in the subsequent social-context speech sample. Such a relation might be expected if crib-speech practice facilitates grammatical development. This relation was found to varying degrees in the speech samples of children A, B, C, F, G, H, J, and L. For these children, the relative fre-

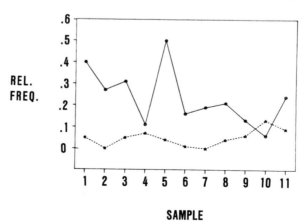

Figure 4-12. Within-sample comparisons of the relative frequency of buildups in the crib speech and social-context speech of Child L. The solid line denotes crib speech. The dashed line denotes social-context speech.

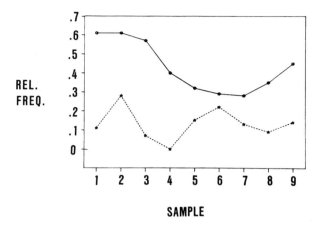

Figure 4-13. Within-sample comparisons of the relative frequency of buildups in the crib speech and social-context speech of Child M. The solid line denotes crib speech. The dashed line denotes social-context speech.

quency of buildups in crib speech was related to subsequent improvements in grammatical development (as measured by MLU). For these children, crib-speech samples in which buildups constituted a large proportion of the children's practice were followed by social-context speech samples in which the children used longer and more complex sentences. Seven of the children (A, C, F, G, H, J, and K) were also more likely to have higher MLUs in social-context speech samples during weeks in which their crib-speech samples contained a large proportion of buildups. Both of these findings provide support for the claim that practice in crib speech facilitates grammatical development, at least insofar as one type of practice (build-ups) is concerned.

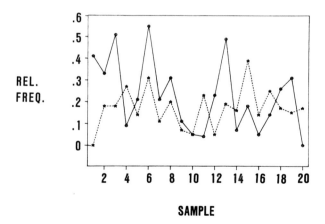

Figure 4-14. Within-sample comparisons of the relative frequency of buildups in the crib speech and social-context speech of Child N. The solid line denotes crib speech. The dashed line denotes social-context speech.

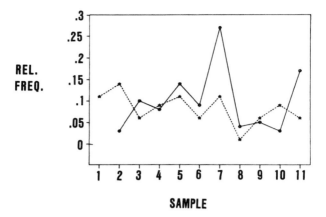

Figure 4-15. Across-sample comparisons of the relative frequency of buildups in the crib speech and social-context speech of Child A. The solid line denotes crib speech. The dashed line denotes social-context speech.

Across-Sample Comparisons

The across-sample comparisons for buildups are shown in Figures 4-15 through 4-28. As was the case for the within-sample comparisons, the relative frequency of buildups was not uniformly distributed across speech samples. Just as there was considerable variability in the proportion of buildups qua linguistic practice, there was also considerable variability in the relative frequency of buildups per sample in the across-sample analyses. If there was no variability, then there would be relative flat lines in the graphs depicting the across-sample comparisons. Such is clearly not the case (see Figures 4-15 through 4-28).

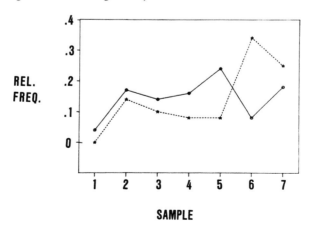

Figure 4-16. Across-sample comparisons of the relative frequency of buildups in the crib speech and social-context speech of Child B. The solid line denotes crib speech. The dashed line denotes social-context speech.

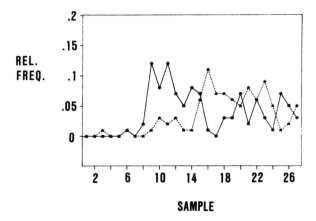

Figure 4-17. Across-sample comparisons of the relative frequency of buildups in the crib speech and social-context speech of Child C. The solid line denotes crib speech. The dashed line denotes social-context speech.

In the within-sample comparisons, it was possible to compare the relative frequencies of buildups in crib speech and in social-context speech in that these relative frequencies reflected the extent to which buildups constituted a proportion of linguistic practice in each speech sample, the possible range being zero to 100% for each sample. It makes less sense to consider the relative frequencies of buildups in the across-sample comparisons in this manner. The across-sample comparisons will always *total* 100% for both crib speech and social-context speech in that the relative frequencies are determined by dividing the number of buildups in one speech sample by the total number of buildups for a particular speech type by a particular

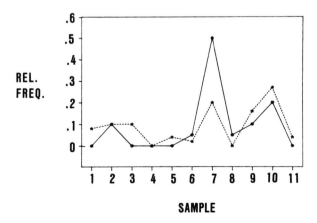

Figure 4-18. Across-sample comparisons of the relative frequency of buildups in the crib speech and social-context speech of Child D. The solid line denotes crib speech. The dashed line denotes social-context speech.

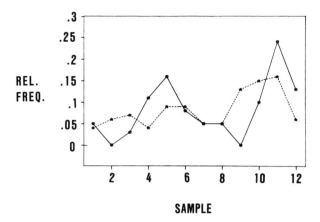

Figure 4-19. Across-sample comparisons of the relative frequency of buildups in the crib speech and social-context speech of Child E. The solid line denotes crib speech. The dashed line denotes social-context speech.

child. Thus, if the relative frequency is high for one sample, it will necessarily be lower for the other samples. As such, comparing the relative frequencies for crib speech and social-context speech should not reveal any consistent pattern in which one type of speech has a higher relative frequency of buildups than the other. This is, in fact, true (see Figures 4-15 through 4-28).

It is possible (and reasonable) to compare the variability of the relative frequencies of buildups in the across-sample comparisons. The variability across samples was not substantially different for crib speech and social-context speech for five of the children (B, C, H, I, and L). This does not mean that there was no variability in the relative frequencies of buildups in crib speech or social-context speech for these

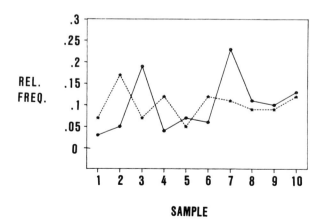

Figure 4-20. Across-sample comparisons of the relative frequency of buildups in the crib speech and social-context speech of Child F. The solid line denotes crib speech. The dashed line denotes social-context speech.

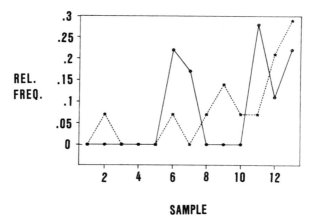

Figure 4-21. Across-sample comparisons of the relative frequency of buildups in the crib speech and social-context speech of Child G. The solid line denotes crib speech. The dashed line denotes social-context speech.

five children, for there most certainly was (see Figures 4-16, 4-17, 4-23, and 4-26). Rather, it means that the amount of variability seemed to be equal for both types of speech samples. Two of the children (K and M; see Figures 4-25 and 4-27) exhibited slightly greater variability for buildups in social-context speech than in crib speech. Variability was greater in crib speech than in social-context speech for the remaining children (A, D, E, F, G, J, and N).

There were few inverse relations between the peaks and valleys of the relative frequencies of buildups across samples in crib speech and in social-context speech. The speech samples of two of the children (D and J) revealed no such relations. The samples of the remaining children revealed at least one inverse relation per child.

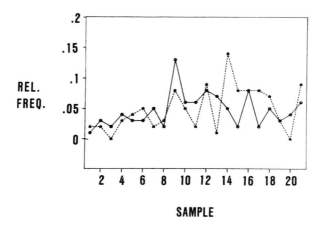

Figure 4-22. Across-sample comparisons of the relative frequency of buildups in the crib speech and social-context speech of Child H. The solid line denotes crib speech. The dashed line denotes social-context speech.

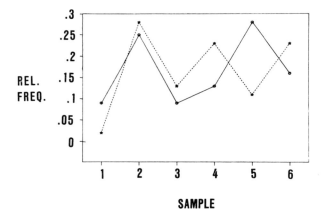

Figure 4-23. Across-sample comparisons of the relative frequency of buildups in the crib speech and social-context speech of Child I. The solid line denotes crib speech. The dashed line denotes social-context speech.

Although the inverse relation between peaks and valleys was found in the across-sample comparisons, the extent of such inverse relations was less than was found in the within-sample comparisons. That the relative frequency of buildups in across-sample comparisons was more likely to vary in the same direction than was the relative frequency of buildups in within-sample comparisons most likely reflects a positive correlation between the use of buildups in crib speech and the use of build-ups in social-context speech. This relation is expressed in the across-sample comparisons rather than in the within-sample comparisons because the across-sample comparisons are concerned with the frequency of buildups in a sample relative to

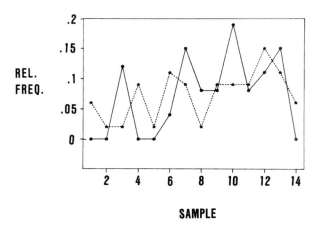

Figure 4-24. Across-sample comparisons of the relative frequency of buildups in the crib speech and social-context speech of Child J. The solid line denotes crib speech. The dashed line denotes social-context speech.

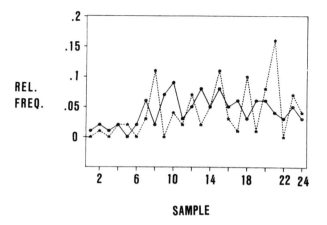

Figure 4-25. Across-sample comparisons of the relative frequency of buildups in the crib speech and social-context speech of Child K. The solid line denotes crib speech. The dashed line denotes social-context speech.

the overall number of buildups produced by the child for a particular type of speech. The within-sample comparisons are concerned with the frequency of build-ups in a speech sample relative to the total number of practice instances for that sample. Buildups might increase in both crib speech and social-context speech from Sample 1 to Sample 2, which would be reflected in the across-sample comparisons. Buildups might nonetheless constitute a larger proportion of the overall practice in crib speech than in social-context speech, and this proportion could vary from sample to sample such that an inverse relation might be found in regard to the within-sample comparisons of crib speech and social-context speech. It is necessary, then,

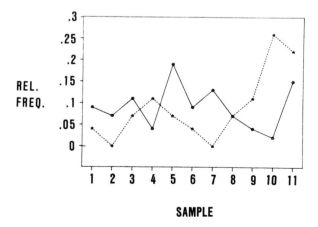

Figure 4-26. Across-sample comparisons of the relative frequency of buildups in the crib speech and social-context speech of Child L. The solid line denotes crib speech. The dashed line denotes social-context speech.

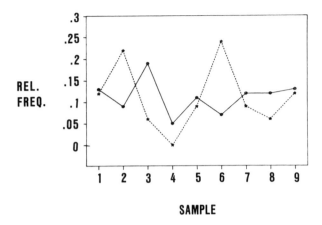

Figure 4-27. Across-sample comparisons of the relative frequency of buildups in the crib speech and social-context speech of Child M. The solid line denotes crib speech. The dashed line denotes social-context speech.

to consider both within-sample and across-sample comparisons in order to ascertain the developmental relations of crib speech and social-context speech in regard to each type of linguistic practice.

Five of the children (B, C, D, L, and M) exhibited patterns in which buildups were more likely to be concentrated in the early crib-speech samples and in the later social-context samples. Three of these children (C, D, and L) revealed the same pattern in the within-sample comparisons. No child exhibited the opposite pattern, these results again supporting the notion that crib speech serves as a trying ground for functions to be later used in social-context speech.

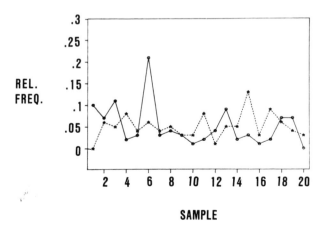

Figure 4-28. Across-sample comparisons of the relative frequency of buildups in the crib speech and social-context speech of Child N. The solid line denotes crib speech. The dashed line denotes social-context speech.

There was a positive relation between the crib-speech MLUs and the relative frequency of crib-speech buildups in the across-sample comparisons for five of the children (B, D, F, G, and I). Two of these children (D and G) exhibited similar positive relations for MLU and relative frequency of buildups in crib speech in the within-sample comparisons. As was the case for the within-sample comparisons, there were no positive relations between MLU and relative frequency of buildups in social-context speech for the across-sample comparisons (with the possible exception of Child B, who exhibited such a positive relation for the early and final samples, but not the ones in between). For some of the children, then, changes in the relative frequency of buildups in the across-sample comparisons were positively related to changes in MLU, but only in crib speech.

Eight of the children (B, D, F, G, I, L, M, and N) exhibited substantial increases in social-context-speech MLU in the samples following a peak in the relative frequency of buildups in a crib-speech sample. This effect was quite evident in the speech samples of five of the children (B, D, F, G, and N) and also apparent in the speech samples of the other three children. Four of these children (B, F, G, and L) exhibited the same relation between social-context-speech MLU and relative frequency of buildups in crib speech in the within-sample comparisons. Child A, who exhibited the relation of a peak in buildups preceding an increase in social-context speech MLU in the within-sample comparisons, exhibited the opposite pattern in the across-sample comparisons. The highest peak in social-context speech MLU precedes the highest peak in crib-speech buildups in these comparisons for Child A. For this child, the relative frequency of buildups across samples in crib speech did not seem to affect social-context speech MLU as much as did the relative frequency of buildups in terms of overall linguistic practice. The significance of this possibility will be discussed in a later section. The speech samples of one child (J) reflected a pattern in which peaks in crib-speech buildups preceded *decreases* in social-context speech MLU. These decreases in social-context speech MLU were followed by increases, and so it is far from clear that buildups did not serve a facilitative function for this child's grammatical development. Six of the children (B, D, E, G, I, and J) exhibited simultaneous increases in crib-speech buildups and in social-context-speech MLU. Only two of these children (G and J) exhibited similar patterns in the within-sample comparisons. Once again, we see a difference between the within- and across-sample comparisons. This finding reflects the difference between the relative frequency of buildups qua linguistic practice and the relative frequency of buildups in a sample compared to the total number of buildups (for a given child).

Comparison of Within- and Across-Sample Comparisons

Comparison of the developmental patterns revealed by the within-sample comparisons and the across-sample comparisons for buildups revealed that the two comparisons tapped similar developmental patterns for social-context speech for all of the children, but only for seven of the children (B, D, E, F, G, J, and L) for crib speech. Moreover, there were some differences in the developmental patterns for five of these children (B, E, F, J, and L). The difference in the similarity of the two types of comparisons for crib speech and for social-context speech will be considered following the presentation of the remainder of the data.

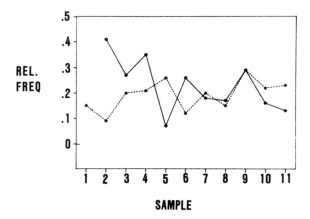

Figure 4-29. Within-sample comparisons of the relative frequency of breakdowns in the crib speech and social-context speech of Child A. The solid line denotes crib speech. The dashed line denotes social-context speech.

Analyses of Developmental Patterns: Breakdowns

Within-Sample Comparisons

The within-sample comparisons are shown in Figures 4-29 through 4-42. Breakdowns comprised a larger proportion of social-context speech practice than crib-speech practice for 11 of the children. This difference was pronounced for nine of the children (B, C, D, E, G, I, J, L, and M), and apparent but less pronounced for the other two children (F and N). There were no substantial differences in the rela-

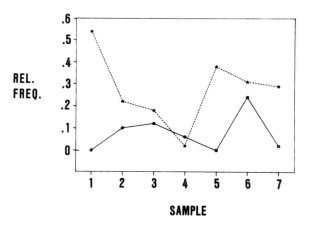

Figure 4-30. Within-sample comparisons of the relative frequency of breakdowns in the crib speech and social-context speech of Child B. The solid line denotes crib speech. The dashed line denotes social-context speech.

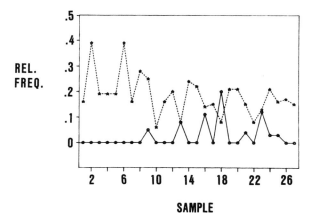

Figure 4-31. Within-sample comparisons of the relative frequency of breakdowns in the crib speech and social-context speech of Child C. The solid line denotes crib speech. The dashed line denotes social-context speech.

tive frequency of breakdowns in the crib speech and in the social-context speech of one child (H). The remaining two children (A and K) exhibited slightly higher relative frequencies for breakdowns in crib speech than in social-context speech.

The within-sample comparisons of relative frequency revealed no instances in which children used a large number of breakdowns in crib speech prior to doing so in social-context speech. Two children (G and M) did use a large proportion of breakdowns in social-context speech prior to doing so in crib speech. These patterns suggest that, contrary to the results found for buildups, breakdowns may be used first in social-context speech and only later used in crib speech.

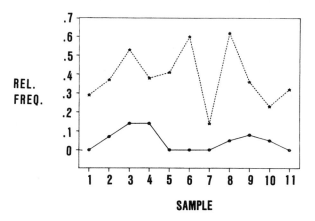

Figure 4-32. Within-sample comparisons of the relative frequency of breakdowns in the crib speech and social-context speech of Child D. The solid line denotes crib speech. The dashed line denotes social-context speech.

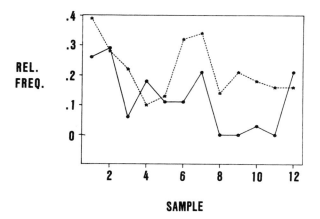

Figure 4-33. Within-sample comparisons of the relative frequency of breakdowns in the crib speech and social-context speech of Child E. The solid line denotes crib speech. The dashed line denotes social-context speech.

The relative frequency of breakdowns was more variable in crib speech than in social-context speech for two children (A and M). The opposite pattern was found for six children (B, C, D, F, G, and J), although the extent of the difference was less for children F and G than for the other four children. There was no real difference in the variability of the relative frequencies of breakdowns in the crib speech and social-context speech of the remaining six children (E, H, I, K, L, and N). With the exception of Child I, there was considerable variability in the relative frequencies of buildups for these six children. However, there was no difference in the degree of variability in the crib-speech samples and the social-context-speech samples.

There were occasional instances of the inverse relation in the peaks and valleys

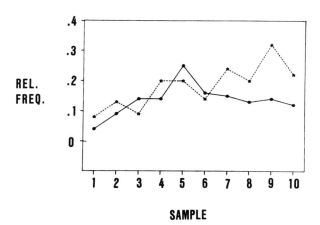

Figure 4-34. Within-sample comparisons of the relative frequency of breakdowns in the crib speech and social-context speech of Child F. The solid line denotes crib speech. The dashed line denotes social-context speech.

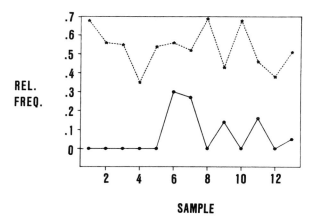

Figure 4-35. Within-sample comparisons of the relative frequency of breakdowns in the crib speech and social-context speech of Child G. The solid line denotes crib speech. The dashed line denotes social-context speech.

of the relative frequencies of breakdowns in crib speech and social-context speech. However, this pattern was most consistently observed in the speech samples of five children (B, C, G, K, and M). For the remaining children, and even occasionally for these five children, the relative frequency of breakdowns was positively rather than negatively related.

There were few positive relations between MLU patterns and within-sample comparisons of breakdowns. One child's (G) crib-speech MLU varied in a similar fashion to the relative frequency of breakdowns in crib speech. Two other children (D and F) exhibited positive relations between social-context-speech MLU and relative frequency of breakdowns in social-context speech.

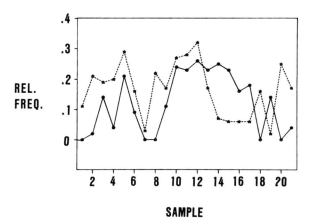

Figure 4-36. Within-sample comparisons of the relative frequency of breakdowns in the crib speech and social-context speech of Child H. The solid line denotes crib speech. The dashed line denotes social-context speech.

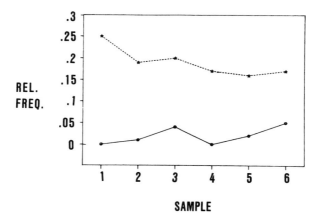

Figure 4-37. Within-sample comparisons of the relative frequency of breakdowns in the crib speech and social-context speech of Child I. The solid line denotes crib speech. The dashed line denotes social-context speech.

Seven of the children (E, F, H, J, K, L, and N) exhibited the following relation between the relative frequency of breakdowns in crib speech and social-context-speech MLU: A peak in the relative frequency of breakdowns in crib speech was followed in the next sample by an increase in social-context-speech MLU. This relation was also occasionally observed in the speech samples of other children but was most evident in the speech of these seven children (less so for children K and L than for children E, F, H, J, and N).

Simultaneous increases in social-context-speech MLU and peaks in the relative frequency of breakdowns in crib speech were observed in the speech samples of seven children (B, C, D, G, H, K, and M). This relation was observed on at least

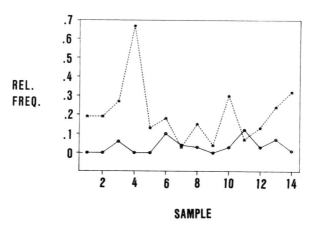

Figure 4-38. Within-sample comparisons of the relative frequency of breakdowns in the crib speech and social-context speech of Child J. The solid line denotes crib speech. The dashed line denotes social-context speech.

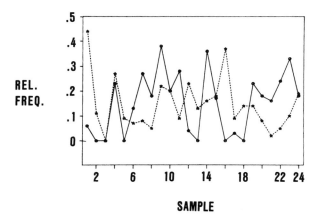

Figure 4-39. Within-sample comparisons of the relative frequency of breakdowns in the crib speech and social-context speech of Child K. The solid line denotes crib speech. The dashed line denotes social-context speech.

several occasions for each of these children and on at least one occasion for four other children (A, F, J, and N). Once again, then, we see a positive relation between a type of practice in crib speech and social-context-speech MLU, either in terms of simultaneous increases in both or an increase in social-context-speech MLU following an increase in crib speech practice.

Across-Sample Comparisons

The across-sample comparisons for breakdowns are shown in Figures 4-43 through 4-56. These comparisons yielded no evidence that the crib-speech setting functioned as a "trying ground" for breakdowns. No child appeared to use crib

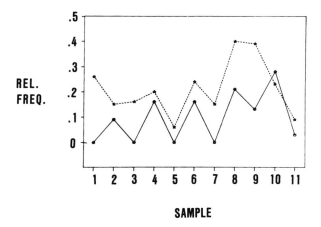

Figure 4-40. Within-sample comparisons of the relative frequency of breakdowns in the crib speech and social-context speech of Child L. The solid line denotes crib speech. The dashed line denotes social-context speech.

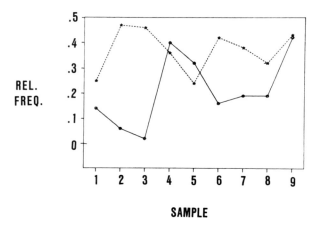

Figure 4-41. Within-sample comparisons of the relative frequency of breakdowns in the crib speech and social-context speech of Child M. The solid line denotes crib speech. The dashed line denotes social-context speech.

speech to learn how to use breakdowns prior to doing so in social-context speech. Two children (G and I), however, did seem to learn to use breakdowns in social-context speech prior to doing so in crib speech. Again, these are not absolute differences, but ones of relative frequency. These results are consistent with those of the within-sample analyses, and suggest that children may learn to use breakdowns in social-context speech and only subsequently come to use breakdowns in crib speech.

The relative frequency of breakdowns was more variable in crib speech than in social-context speech for 11 of the 14 children (B, C, D, E, F, G, I, J, L, M, and N). This difference was substantial for five of the children (C, D, G, I, and J) and slight for six of the children (B, E, F, L, M, and N). There was no difference in overall

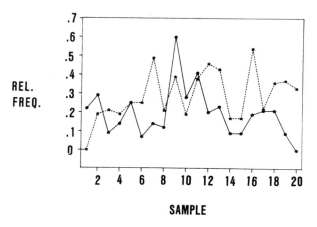

Figure 4-42. Within-sample comparisons of the relative frequency of breakdowns in the crib speech and social-context speech of Child N. The solid line denotes crib speech. The dashed line denotes social-context speech.

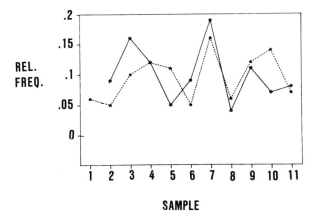

Figure 4-43. Across-sample comparisons of the relative frequency of breakdowns in the crib speech and social-context speech of Child A. The solid line denotes crib speech. The dashed line denotes social-context speech.

variability for the other three children (A, H, and K). Again, this does not mean that there was no variability in the relative frequency of breakdowns in crib speech and in social-context speech, but instead that the relative frequency of breakdowns in each type of speech sample was equally variable. Although there were occasional instances of an inverse relation between the peaks and valleys in the relative frequency of breakdowns in crib speech and social-context speech, the more frequent pattern was one in which the relative frequency of breakdowns in the two types of speech samples varied in the same direction from sample to sample.

No child exhibited a positive relation between MLU and the relative frequency of breakdowns in social-context speech. Two children (G and M) did exhibit similar

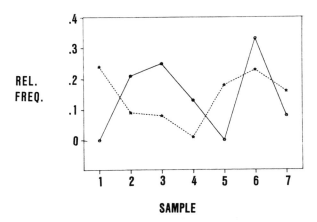

Figure 4-44. Across-sample comparisons of the relative frequency of breakdowns in the crib speech and social-context speech of Child B. The solid line denotes crib speech. The dashed line denotes social-context speech.

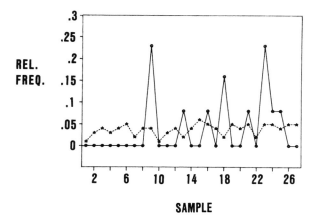

Figure 4-45. Across-sample comparisons of the relative frequency of breakdowns in the crib speech and social-context speech of Child C. The solid line denotes crib speech. The dashed line denotes social-context speech.

developmental patterns between MLU and the relative frequency of breakdowns in crib speech. Ten of the children (B, C, D, E, F, G, I, J, L, and N) exhibited increases in social-context-speech MLU following peaks in the relative frequency of buildups in crib speech. Six children (A, B, G, H, I, and L), including three of the ten children just mentioned, exhibited an increase in social-context-speech MLU simultaneously with a peak in the relative frequency of breakdowns in crib speech. Once again, then, practice in crib speech was positively related to social-context-speech MLU.

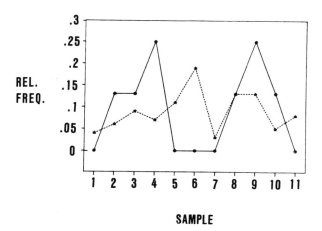

Figure 4-46. Across-sample comparisons of the relative frequency of breakdowns in the crib speech and social-context speech of Child D. The solid line denotes crib speech. The dashed line denotes social-context speech.

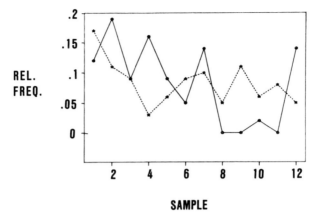

Figure 4-47. Across-sample comparisons of the relative frequency of breakdowns in the crib speech and social-context speech of Child E. The solid line denotes crib speech. The dashed line denotes social-context speech.

Comparison of Within-Sample and Across-Sample Comparisons

The within-sample and across-sample comparisons revealed similar overall developmental patterns for social-context speech for three of the children (A, B, and M) and for crib speech for eight of the children (B, C, D, E, G, H, J, and L). For each of these children, the two types of comparisons yielded similar developmental trends. However, it is important to remember that these similarities are for the two types of comparisons for each child, not similarities of the children as a group.

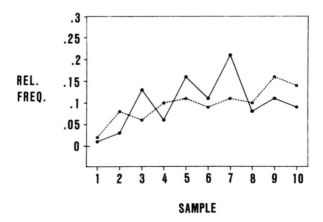

Figure 4-48. Across-sample comparisons of the relative frequency of breakdowns in the crib speech and social-context speech of Child F. The solid line denotes crib speech. The dashed line denotes social-context speech.

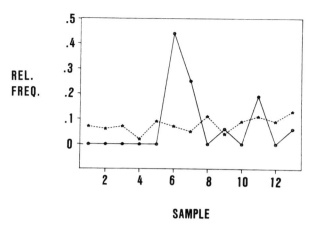

Figure 4-49. Across-sample comparisons of the relative frequency of breakdowns in the crib speech and social-context speech of Child G. The solid line denotes crib speech. The dashed line denotes social-context speech.

Analyses of Developmental Patterns: Completions

Within-Sample Comparisons

The results of the within-sample comparisons are shown in Figures 4-57 through 4-70. Completions consistently comprised a larger proportion of linguistic practice in crib speech than in social-context speech for six of the children (B, C, F, H, L, and N). The opposite pattern held for five of the remaining children (D, G, I, J, and M). Completions comprised a low proportion of linguistic practice in both crib speech and social-context speech for two of these children (G and J). In fact, there

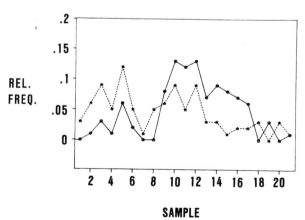

Figure 4-50. Across-sample comparisons of the relative frequency of breakdowns in the crib speech and social-context speech of Child H. The solid line denotes crib speech. The dashed line denotes social-context speech.

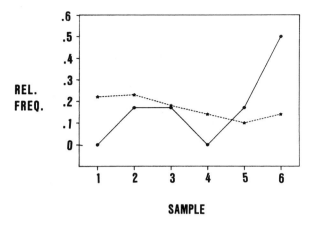

Figure 4-51. Across-sample comparisons of the relative frequency of breakdowns in the crib speech and social-context speech of Child I. The solid line denotes crib speech. The dashed line denotes social-context speech.

were *no* instances of completions in the crib speech of Child J. There were no substantial differences in the within-sample relative frequencies of completions in crib speech and social-context speech for the remaining three children (A, E, and K).

One child (A) used completions more frequently (relative to the total amount of linguistic practice) in crib speech than in social-context speech in the early samples, the opposite pattern holding for the later samples. This suggests that Child A may have been using crib speech to consolidate the use of completions as a form of linguistic practice. After this consolidation took place, completions comprised a larger proportion of Child A's social-context-speech linguistic practice. Even though completions in social-context speech may function as a communicative device as well as

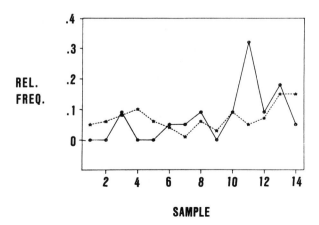

Figure 4-52. Across-sample comparisons of the relative frequency of breakdowns in the crib speech and social-context speech of Child J. The solid line denotes crib speech. The dashed line denotes social-context speech.

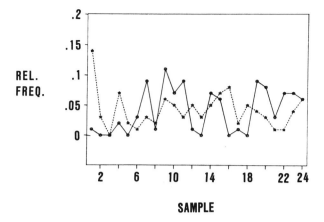

REL.
FREQ.

SAMPLE

Figure 4-53. Across-sample comparisons of the relative frequency of breakdowns in the crib speech and social-context speech of Child K. The solid line denotes crib speech. The dashed line denotes social-context speech.

a practice device, Child A seemed to use crib speech as a context in which to learn to use completions. Children, then, may use crib speech to learn how to practice, what to practice, and alternative uses of practice types.

Opposite the pattern reflected by Child A, children C, D, and G appeared to have learned to use completions in social-context speech prior to learning to do so in crib speech. This pattern held for Child G, but Child G infrequently employed completions in either crib speech or social-context speech. Similarly, the difference was relatively slight in the speech of Child C (in the early samples). However, the early emergence of completions in social-context speech is readily apparent in the speech

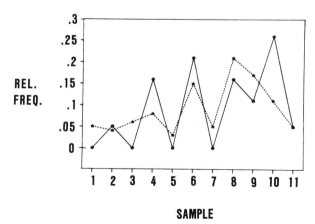

REL.
FREQ.

SAMPLE

Figure 4-54. Across-sample comparisons of the relative frequency of breakdowns in the crib speech and social-context speech of Child L. The solid line denotes crib speech. The dashed line denotes social-context speech.

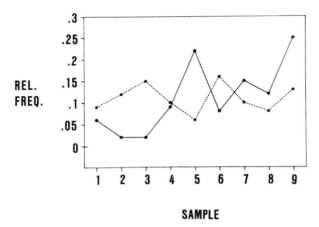

Figure 4-55. Across-sample comparisons of the relative frequency of breakdowns in the crib speech and social-context speech of Child M. The solid line denotes crib speech. The dashed line denotes social-context speech.

samples of Child D. This child appeared to have learned to use completions in social-context speech at least 7 weeks prior to their emergence in crib speech.

The proportion of completions in regard to overall linguistic practice was more variable in crib speech than in social-context speech for eight of the children (A, C, E, F, H, K, L, and N), but more variable in social-context speech than in crib speech for two of the children (D and J). However, it must be remembered that Child J produced no completions in crib speech. There was no difference in the amount of variability of completions in crib speech and in social-context speech for the remaining children (B, G, I, and M). A peak in the relative frequency of comple-

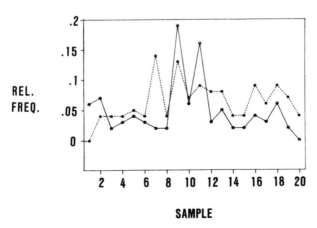

Figure 4-56. Across-sample comparisons of the relative frequency of breakdowns in the crib speech and social-context speech of Child N. The solid line denotes crib speech. The dashed line denotes social-context speech.

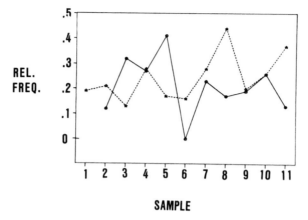

Figure 4-57. Within-sample comparisons of the relative frequency of completions in the crib speech and social-context speech of Child A. The solid line denotes crib speech. The dashed line denotes social-context speech.

tions in crib speech tended to coincide with a dip in the relative frequency of completions in social-context speech and vice versa for three of the children (F, K, and N). Similar inverse relations were found in the speech samples of two other children (B and E), although not to the extent of the other three children (F, K, and N).

No child exhibited similar overall developmental patterns between the relative frequency of completions and MLU in social-context speech. There were similar overall developmental patterns between the relative frequency of completions and MLU in crib speech for three of the children (B, E, and H). Although these were the only overall developmental similarities, there were many partial similarities (in terms of week-to-week variation) in both the crib-speech and social-context-speech

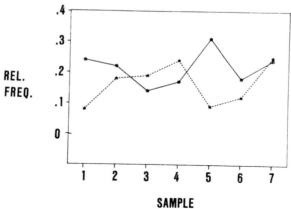

Figure 4-58. Within-sample comparisons of the relative frequency of completions in the crib speech and social-context speech of Child B. The solid line denotes crib speech. The dashed line denotes social-context speech.

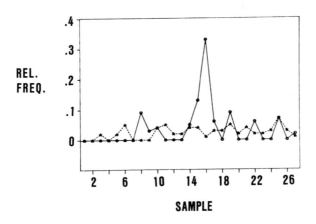

Figure 4-59. Within-sample comparisons of the relative frequency of completions in the crib speech and social-context speech of Child C. The solid line denotes crib speech. The dashed line denotes social-context speech.

MLUs. Five of the children (A, B, D, F, and H) had increases in social-context-speech MLU following peaks in the relative frequency of completions in crib speech. There were increases in social-context-speech MLU simultaneously with peaks in the relative frequency of completions for seven of the children (A, C, E, F, K, L, and N). The use of completions in crib speech, then, was positively related to increases in social-context-speech MLU.

Across-Sample Comparisons

The results of the across-sample comparisons are shown in Figures 4-71 through 4-85. Comparing the relative frequencies of completions revealed no cases in which

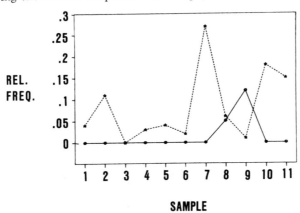

Figure 4-60. Within-sample comparisons of the relative frequency of completions in the crib speech and social-context speech of Child D. The solid line denotes crib speech. The dashed line denotes social-context speech.

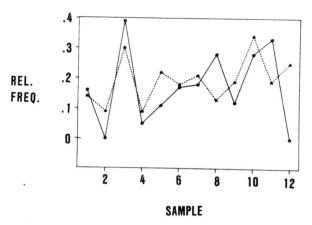

Figure 4-61. Within-sample comparisons of the relative frequency of completions in the crib speech and social-context speech of Child E. The solid line denotes crib speech. The dashed line denotes social-context speech.

a child seemed to learn to use completions in crib speech prior to doing so in social-context speech. Four children (C, D, G, and H) used completions in social-context speech prior to doing so in crib speech and as such seem to have used the social-context-speech setting to master the use of completions and later used this sort of practice in crib speech to further their language development. (Child J used completions only in the social-context-speech setting.)

There was greater variability in the relative frequency of completions in crib speech than in social-context speech for eight of the children (A, B, C, D, E, G, I, and M). Two children (J and L) showed greater variability in their use of comple-

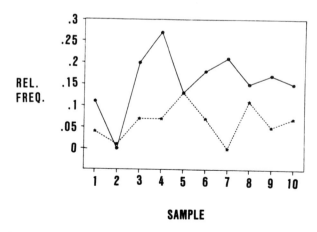

Figure 4-62. Within-sample comparisons of the relative frequency of completions in the crib speech and social-context speech of Child F. The solid line denotes crib speech. The dashed line denotes social-context speech.

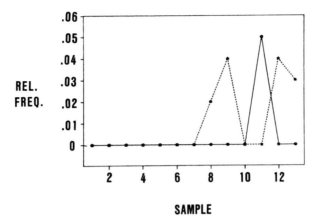

Figure 4-63. Within-sample comparisons of the relative frequency of completions in the crib speech and social-context speech of Child G. The solid line denotes crib speech. The dashed line denotes social-context speech.

tions in social-context speech than in crib speech (Child J used no completions in crib speech). There was little difference in the amount of variability of completions in crib speech and social-context speech for four children (F, H, K, and N).

There were inverse relations between the peaks and valleys of relative frequencies of completions in crib speech and social-context speech for ten of the children (A, B, D, E, F, H, I, K, L, and N). For these children, a peak in the relative frequency of completions in crib speech tended to correspond to a dip in the relative frequencies of completions in social-context speech, and vice versa. This relation was occasionally observed in the speech samples of five of the children (A, E, H, I,

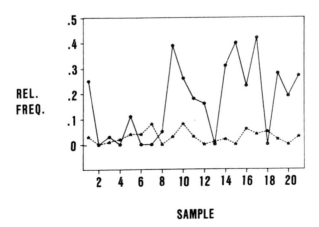

Figure 4-64. Within-sample comparisons of the relative frequency of completions in the crib speech and social-context speech of Child H. The solid line denotes crib speech. The dashed line denotes social-context speech.

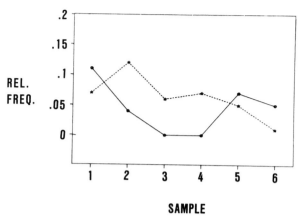

SAMPLE

Figure 4-65. Within-sample comparisons of the relative frequency of completions in the crib speech and social-context speech of Child I. The solid line denotes crib speech. The dashed line denotes social-context speech.

and L) and frequently observed in the speech samples of the other five children (B, D, F, K, and N).

Three children (B, E, and H) exhibited similar developmental patterns for MLU and relative frequency of completions across samples in crib speech. There were also similar developmental patterns for MLU and relative frequency of completions in the crib speech of children H and L (except for the last crib-speech sample for each child), and for the peaks in the middle crib-speech samples for Child C. Two children (B and L) exhibited similar developmental patterns for MLU and relative

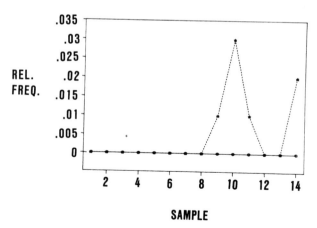

SAMPLE

Figure 4-66. Within-sample comparisons of the relative frequency of completions in the crib speech and social-context speech of Child J. The solid line denotes crib speech. The dashed line denotes social-context speech.

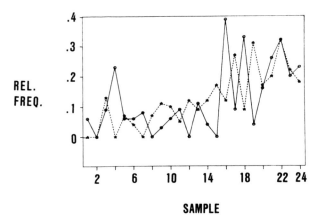

Figure 4-67. Within-sample comparisons of the relative frequency of completions in the crib speech and social-context speech of Child K. The solid line denotes crib speech. The dashed line denotes social-context speech.

frequency of completions across samples in social-context speech, as did Child F with the exception of the last social-context speech sample.

There were increases in social-context-speech MLU that corresponded with peaks in the relative frequency of completions in crib speech for four of the children (E, H, L, and N). Increases in social-context speech MLU that followed peaks in the use of completions in crib speech were consistently observed in the speech samples of six children (B, D, F, G, H, and M) and in the early speech samples of another child (C). Another child (I) exhibited a simultaneous increase in social-context-speech

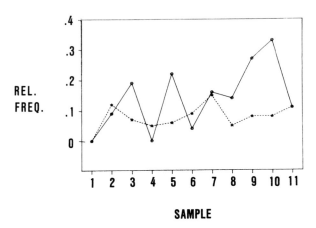

Figure 4-68. Within-sample comparisons of the relative frequency of completions in the crib speech and social-context speech of Child L. The solid line denotes crib speech. The dashed line denotes social-context speech.

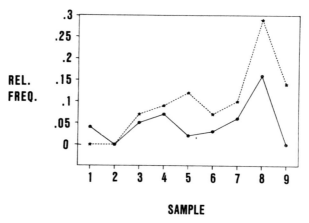

SAMPLE

Figure 4-69. Within-sample comparisons of the relative frequency of completions in the crib speech and social-context speech of Child M. The solid line denotes crib speech. The dashed line denotes social-context speech.

MLU with the earliest peak in the use of completions in crib speech and an increase in social-context-speech MLU following the last peak in use of completions in crib speech. Here, then, is further support for the notion that practice in crib speech facilitates grammatical development.

Comparison of Within-Sample and Across-Sample Comparisons

There were similar developmental patterns revealed in the within-sample comparisons and across-sample comparisons for completions in crib speech for seven of the children (A, B, C, D, I, M, and N). There were also similar developmental patterns

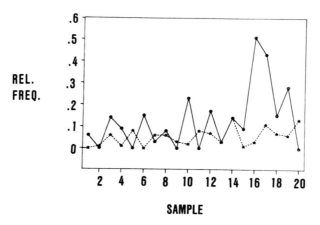

SAMPLE

Figure 4-70. Within-sample comparisons of the relative frequency of completions in the crib speech and social-context speech of Child N. The solid line denotes crib speech. The dashed line denotes social-context speech.

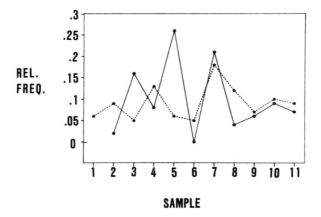

Figure 4-71. Across-sample comparisons of the relative frequency of completions in the crib speech and social-context speech of Child A. The solid line denotes crib speech. The dashed line denotes social-context speech.

in the within-sample comparisons and across-sample comparisons in the social-context speech of nine children (A, B, C, D, F, H, I, M, and N).

Analyses of Developmental Patterns: Exact Reproductions

Within-Sample Comparisons

The relative frequencies of exact reproductions were higher in crib speech than in social-context speech for five of the children (C, D, E, G, and J)(see Figures 4-84

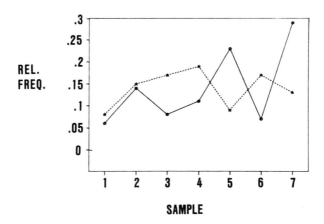

Figure 4-72. Across-sample comparisons of the relative frequency of completions in the crib speech and social-context speech of Child B. The solid line denotes crib speech. The dashed line denotes social-context speech.

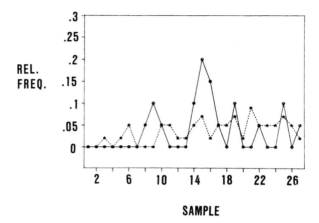

SAMPLE

Figure 4-73. Across-sample comparisons of the relative frequency of completions in the crib speech and social-context speech of Child C. The solid line denotes crib speech. The dashed line denotes social-context speech.

through 4-98). The opposite pattern held for seven of the remaining children (A, B, F, H, K, L, and M). There was no substantial difference in the relative frequencies of exact reproductions in the crib-speech samples and social-context-speech samples for the remaining two children (I and N). There were only two instances in which a child seemed to acquire the use of exact reproductions in one speech setting before doing so in the other speech setting. Child C used exact reproductions in crib speech prior to doing so in social-context speech. Child A exhibited the opposite pattern. Child N used exact reproductions in social-context speech to a much

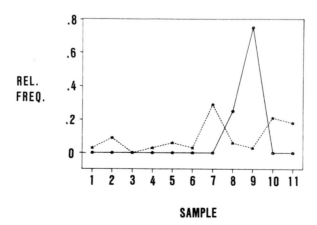

SAMPLE

Figure 4-74. Across-sample comparisons of the relative frequency of completions in the crib speech and social-context speech of Child D. The solid line denotes crib speech. The dashed line denotes social-context speech.

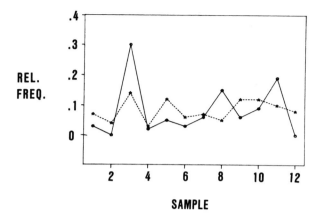

REL.
FREQ.

SAMPLE

Figure 4-75. Across-sample comparisons of the relative frequency of completions in the crib speech and social-context speech of Child E. The solid line denotes crib speech. The dashed line denotes social-context speech.

greater extent than in crib speech for the first two samples, after which a much more variable pattern emerged. Of course, these patterns reflect the relative frequency of exact reproductions in regard to the overall amount of linguistic practice. The across-sample comparisons will provide additional information concerning this matter.

There was no significant difference in the extent of variability of the relative frequencies of exact reproductions in the crib-speech samples and in the social-context-speech samples for seven of the children (A, B, F, I, L, M, and N). The rela-

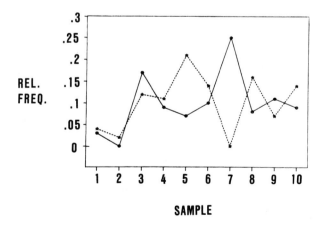

REL.
FREQ.

SAMPLE

Figure 4-76. Across-sample comparisons of the relative frequency of completions in the crib speech and social-context speech of Child F. The solid line denotes crib speech. The dashed line denotes social-context speech.

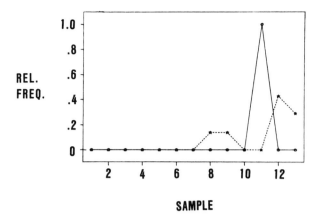

Figure 4-77. Across-sample comparisons of the relative frequency of completions in the crib speech and social-context speech of Child G. The solid line denotes crib speech. The dashed line denotes social-context speech.

tive frequency of exact reproductions evidenced greater variability in social-context speech than in crib speech for one child (J). The opposite pattern held for the remaining six children (C, D, E, G, H, and K). There was an inverse relation in the peaks and valleys of the relative frequencies of exact reproductions in the crib-speech samples and in the social-context speech samples of five of the children (A, G, I, J, and M). For these children, a peak in the relative frequency of exact reproductions in crib speech tended to correspond to a dip in the relative frequency of exact reproductions in social-context speech, and vice versa. This pattern was

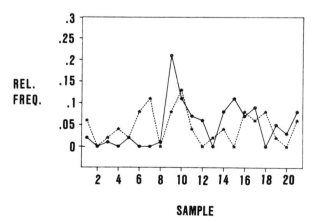

Figure 4-78. Across-sample comparisons of the relative frequency of completions in the crib speech and social-context speech of Child H. The solid line denotes crib speech. The dashed line denotes social-context speech.

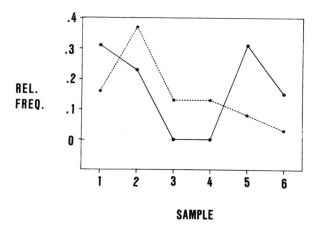

Figure 4-79. Across-sample comparisons of the relative frequency of completions in the crib speech and social-context speech of Child I. The solid line denotes crib speech. The dashed line denotes social-context speech.

also usually observed in the speech samples of Child K, observed in the first eight samples (but not the last three samples) of Child L, in the middle samples of Child D, occasionally in the speech samples of Child N, in the first crib-speech and social-context-speech sample of Child B, and the last speech samples of children C and E.

There were very few instances in which there were similar developmental patterns in children's MLU and the relative frequency of exact reproductions in the within-sample comparisons. There was a fairly good correspondence between the developmental patterns of the relative frequency of exact reproductions and MLU

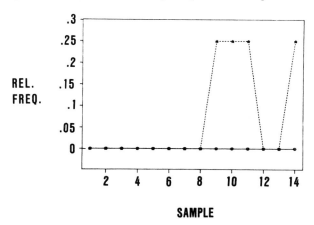

Figure 4-80. Across-sample comparisons of the relative frequency of completions in the crib speech and social-context speech of Child J. The solid line denotes crib speech. The dashed line denotes social-context speech.

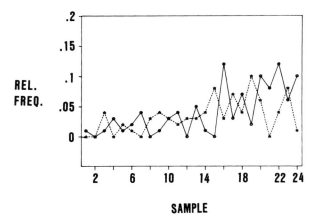

Figure 4-81. Across-sample comparisons of the relative frequency of completions in the crib speech and social-context speech of Child K. The solid line denotes crib speech. The dashed line denotes social-context speech.

in the crib speech of Child L. This was also true for the early crib-speech samples of Child I and the middle crib-speech samples of Child M. There were similar developmental patterns in the MLUs and relative frequencies of exact reproductions in the social-context speech of Child M. This was also true for the later social-context-speech samples of Child I. For the remaining children, if there was any relation, it seemed to be a negative relation between MLU and the relative frequency of exact reproductions, where a dip in the relative frequency of exact reproductions corresponded with an increase in MLU, and vice versa.

Peaks in the relative frequency of exact reproductions in crib speech were fol-

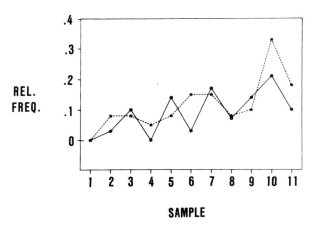

Figure 4-82. Across-sample comparisons of the relative frequency of completions in the crib speech and social-context speech of Child L. The solid line denotes crib speech. The dashed line denotes social-context speech.

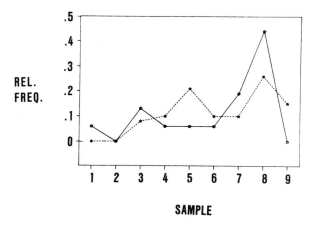

Figure 4-83. Across-sample comparisons of the relative frequency of completions in the crib speech and social-context speech of Child M. The solid line denotes crib speech. The dashed line denotes social-context speech.

lowed (at least occasionally) by increases in social-context-speech MLU in the speech samples of each of the children. Peaks in the relative frequency of exact reproductions in crib speech were associated with simultaneous increases in social-context-speech MLU (at least occasionally) in the speech samples of nine of the children (A, B, C, D, F, H, J, K, and L).

Across-Sample Comparisons

The across-sample comparisons yielded no instances in which one type of speech (crib or social-context) seemed to serve as a trying ground for the use of exact

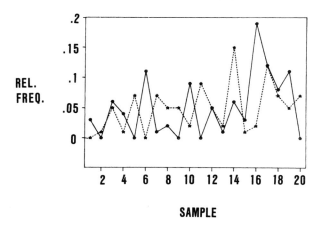

Figure 4-84. Across-sample comparisons of the relative frequency of completions in the crib speech and social-context speech of Child N. The solid line denotes crib speech. The dashed line denotes social-context speech.

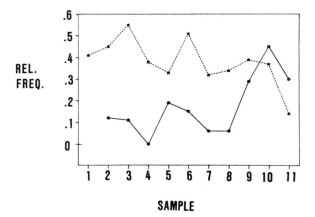

Figure 4-85. Within-sample comparisons of the relative frequency of exact reproductions in the crib speech and social-context speech of Child A. The solid line denotes crib speech. The dashed line denotes social-context speech.

reproductions prior to the use of the same type of practice in the other type of speech. (See Figures 4-99 through 4-112.) This does not mean that the relative frequencies of exact reproductions did not vary in a different fashion in crib speech than in social-context speech, but rather that children did not seem to favor either type of speech as the appropriate learning climate for exact reproductions.

No child exhibited greater variability in the amount of variability in exact reproductions in social-context speech than in crib speech. There was more variability in the amount of variability in the crib-speech samples than in the social-context-

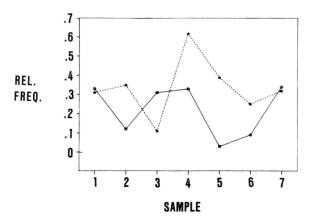

Figure 4-86. Within-sample comparisons of the relative frequency of exact reproductions in the crib speech and social-context speech of Child B. The solid line denotes crib speech. The dashed line denotes social-context speech.

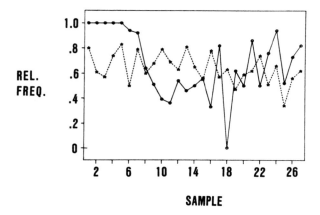

SAMPLE

Figure 4-87. Within-sample comparisons of the relative frequency of exact reproductions in the crib speech and social-context speech of Child C. The solid line
denotes crib speech. The dashed line denotes social-context speech.

speech samples for four of the children (A, B, I, and M). Another child (K) exhibited this same pattern, but to a much lesser extent than did children A, B, I, and
M. There was no substantial difference between crib speech and social-context
speech in degree of variability of the relative frequencies of exact reproductions in
the speech of the remaining nine children (C, D, E, F, G, H, J, L, and N).

   Although there were inverse relations between the peaks and dips of relative frequencies of exact reproductions in the speech samples of nine of the children (A, B,
C, F, H, J, K, L, and M), the peaks and valleys were not very dramatic and so

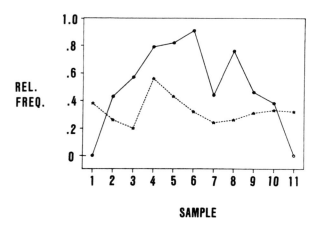

SAMPLE

Figure 4-88. Within-sample comparisons of the relative frequency of exact reproductions in the crib speech and social-context speech of Child D. The solid line
denotes crib speech. The dashed line denotes social-context speech.

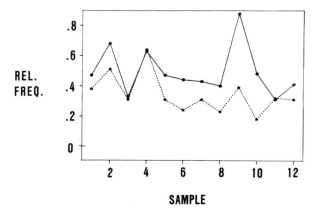

Figure 4-89. Within-sample comparisons of the relative frequency of exact reproductions in the crib speech and social-context speech of Child E. The solid line
denotes crib speech. The dashed line denotes social-context speech.

neither are the inverse relations (the one exception occurring in crib-speech and
social-context-speech Samples 3–5 for Child M). Only one child (I) exhibited similar
overall developmental patterns in the relative frequencies of exact reproductions
and MLU. This was only true for the crib-speech samples. Exact reproductions,
then, tended to not mirror the developmental course of MLU. There were relatively
few peaks in the relative frequencies of exact reproductions in the crib speech of
the 14 children. Nonetheless, these peaks corresponded to simultaneous increases in
social-context-speech MLU for six children (A, B, D, G, I, and M) and to increases

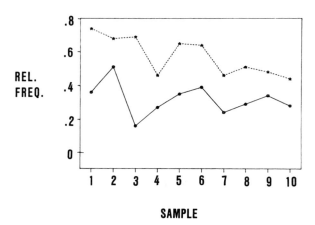

Figure 4-90. Within-sample comparisons of the relative frequency of exact reproductions in the crib speech and social-context speech of Child F. The solid line
denotes crib speech. The dashed line denotes social-context speech.

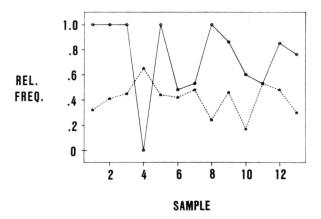

Figure 4-91. Within-sample comparisons of the relative frequency of exact reproductions in the crib speech and social-context speech of Child G. The solid line denotes crib speech. The dashed line denotes social-context speech.

in the subsequent social-context-speech-sample MLU for eight of the children (A, B, D, F, G, I, M, and N). This once again suggests that practice in crib speech may facilitate grammatical development and its productive use in social-context speech.

Comparison of Within-Sample and Across-Sample Comparisons

Child M was the only child to exhibit similar developmental patterns in the within-sample and across-sample comparisons of the relative frequency of exact reproductions in social-context speech. Child M and two other children (B and I) had

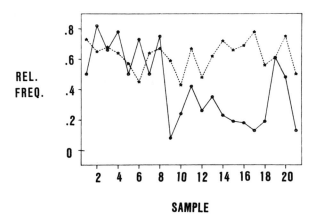

Figure 4-92. Within-sample comparisons of the relative frequency of exact reproductions in the crib speech and social-context speech of Child H. The solid line denotes crib speech. The dashed line denotes social-context speech.

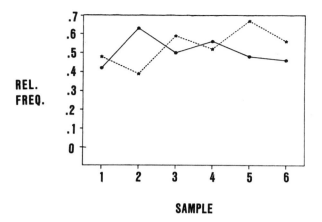

Figure 4-93. Within-sample comparisons of the relative frequency of exact reproductions in the crib speech and social-context speech of Child I. The solid line
denotes crib speech. The dashed line denotes social-context speech.

similar developmental patterns in the two types of comparisons in crib speech
(there was one discrepancy in the two patterns for Child I; this occurred in the fifth
crib-speech sample).

Analyses of Developmental Patterns: Substitutions

Within-Sample Comparisons

The results of the within-sample comparisons of the relative frequency of substitutions are shown in Figures 4-113 through 4-126. For 11 of the children (A, B, D,

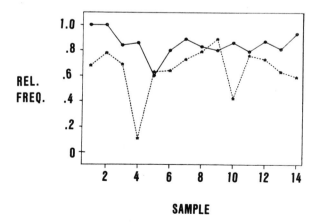

Figure 4-94. Within-sample comparisons of the relative frequency of exact reproductions in the crib speech and social-context speech of Child J. The solid line
denotes crib speech. The dashed line denotes social-context speech.

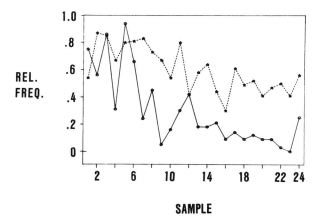

Figure 4-95. Within-sample comparisons of the relative frequency of exact reproductions in the crib speech and social-context speech of Child K. The solid line denotes crib speech. The dashed line denotes social-context speech.

E, G, I, J, K, L, M, and N), substitutions consistently comprised a greater proportion of practice in crib speech than in social-context speech. There was one significant deviation from this pattern for Child B in the third crib-speech and social-context-speech samples. Nonetheless, in general Child B seemed more likely to use substitutions in crib speech than in social-context speech. The remaining three children (C, F, and H) exhibited little if any difference in the relative use of substitutions in crib speech and social-context speech.

One child (H) appeared to use completions in social-context speech prior to doing so in crib speech. Two children (C and F) exhibited the opposite pattern. The relative frequency of substitutions was more variable in crib speech than in social-

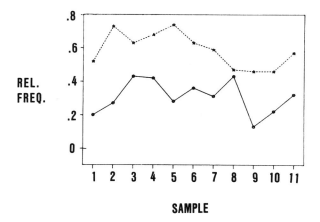

Figure 4-96. Within-sample comparisons of the relative frequency of exact reproductions in the crib speech and social-context speech of Child L. The solid line denotes crib speech. The dashed line denotes social-context speech.

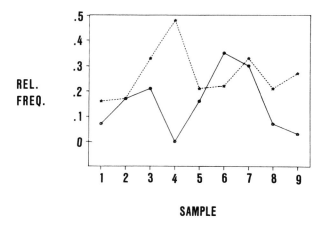

Figure 4-97. Within-sample comparisons of the relative frequency of exact reproductions in the crib speech and social-context speech of Child M. The solid line denotes crib speech. The dashed line denotes social-context speech.

context speech for nine children (A, D, E, G, I, J, K, L, and N). The opposite pattern held for two children (B and F). There was not a substantial difference in the degree of variability of substitutions in the speech samples of the remaining three children (C, H, and M). There was a tendency for a dip in the relative frequency of substitutions in crib speech to correspond to a peak (or increase) in the relative frequency of substitutions in social-context speech, and vice versa, for seven of the children (B, C, D, H, I, K, and L). This pattern was not absolute for these children, but rather a tendency.

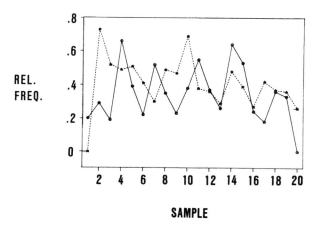

Figure 4-98. Within-sample comparisons of the relative frequency of exact reproductions in the crib speech and social-context speech of Child N. The solid line denotes crib speech. The dashed line denotes social-context speech.

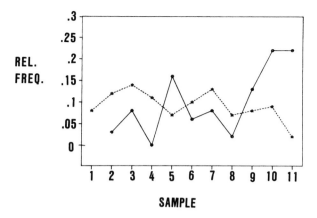

Figure 4-99. Across-sample comparisons of the relative frequency of exact reproductions in the crib speech and social-context speech of Child A. The solid line denotes crib speech. The dashed line denotes social-context speech.

There was only one case in which changes in a child's MLU paralleled changes in the relative frequency of substitutions across samples. This occurred for Child K's crib-speech samples. Even here, the relation was not perfect, but there was a considerable amount of similarity. Nonetheless, it should be kept in mind that this relation was found in the speech of only one child, and only for crib speech. For this child, increases or decreases in MLU paralleled increases or decreases in the relative frequency of substitutions (in crib speech).

A peak in the relative frequency of substitutions in crib speech was associated

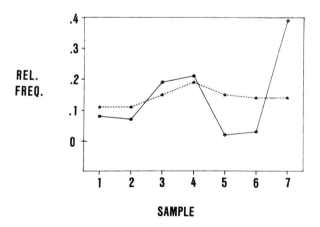

Figure 4-100. Across-sample comparisons of the relative frequency of exact reproductions in the crib speech and social-context speech of Child B. The solid line denotes crib speech. The dashed line denotes social-context speech.

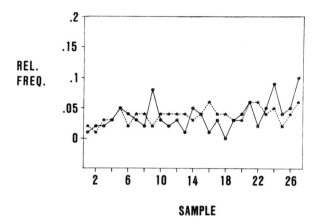

Figure 4-101. Across-sample comparisons of the relative frequency of exact reproductions in the crib speech and social-context speech of Child C. The solid line denotes crib speech. The dashed line denotes social-context speech.

with a simultaneous increase in social-context-speech MLU for seven of the children (A, C, E, H, I, L, and N). A peak in the relative frequency of substitutions in crib speech was followed by an increase in social-context speech for 11 of the children (B, C, D, G, H, I, J, K, L, M, and N). The use of substitutions in crib speech seemed to be related to grammatical development (as assessed by MLU) for these children.

Across-Sample Comparisons

The results of the across-sample comparisons are summarized in Figures 4-127 through 4-140. One child (H) appeared to learn to use substitutions in social-

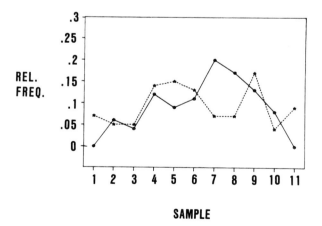

Figure 4-102. Across-sample comparisons of the relative frequency of exact reproductions in the crib speech and social-context speech of Child D. The solid line denotes crib speech. The dashed line denotes social-context speech.

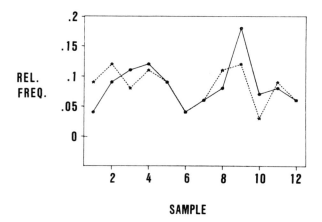

Figure 4-103. Across-sample comparisons of the relative frequency of exact reproductions in the crib speech and social-context speech of Child E. The solid line
denotes crib speech. The dashed line denotes social-context speech.

context speech prior to doing so in crib speech. Two children (G and N) appeared
to learn to use substitutions in crib speech prior to doing so in social-context
speech. The relative frequency of substitutions across samples proved to be more
variable in crib speech than in social-context speech for four children (A, C, D, and
G). The opposite pattern held for one child (I). There was no difference in the
extent of variability in the crib-speech and social-context-speech samples for the
remaining nine children (B, E, F, H, J, K, L, M, and N). An inverse relation between
the peaks and dips in the relative frequencies of substitutions in crib speech and in
social-context speech was found in the speech samples of five of the children (A, B,

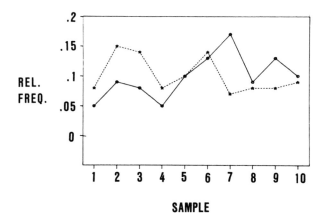

Figure 4-104. Across-sample comparisons of the relative frequency of exact reproductions in the crib speech and social-context speech of Child F. The solid line
denotes crib speech. The dashed line denotes social-context speech.

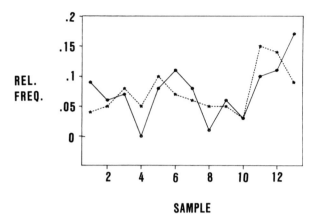

Figure 4-105. Across-sample comparisons of the relative frequency of exact reproductions in the crib speech and social-context speech of Child G. The solid line
denotes crib speech. The dashed line denotes social-context speech.

C, I, and L). For these children, a dip in the relative frequency of substitutions in
crib speech tended to correspond with a peak (or increase) in the relative frequency
of substitutions in social-context speech, and vice versa.

One child (E) exhibited similar developmental patterns for the relative frequency
of substitutions and MLU in social-context speech. Four children (B, D, F, and M)
exhibited similar developmental patterns for the relative frequency of substitutions
and MLU in crib speech (this was true for all but the last speech samples of Child
M). For two children (E and I), peaks in the relative frequency of substitutions in
crib speech corresponded with simultaneous increases in social-context-speech

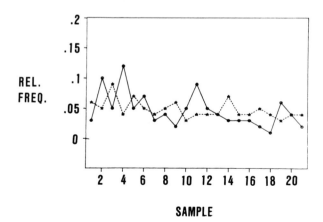

Figure 4-106. Across-sample comparisons of the relative frequency of exact reproductions in the crib speech and social-context speech of Child H. The solid line
denotes crib speech. The dashed line denotes social-context speech.

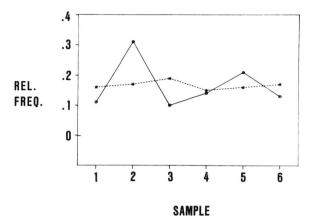

Figure 4-107. Across-sample comparisons of the relative frequency of exact reproductions in the crib speech and social-context speech of Child I. The solid line denotes crib speech. The dashed line denotes social-context speech.

MLU. Peaks in the relative frequency of substitutions in crib speech were followed by increases in social-context speech MLU for ten of the children (B, C, D, F, G, H, J, K, M, and N). This is further support for the claim that crib-speech practice facilitates grammatical development.

Comparisons of Within-Sample and Across-Sample Analyses

There were similar developmental patterns between the within-sample and across-sample comparisons of substitutions for crib speech for four of the children (E, G,

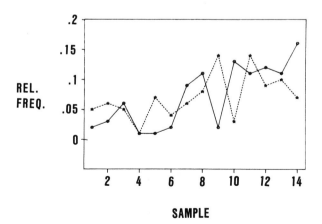

Figure 4-108. Across-sample comparisons of the relative frequency of exact reproductions in the crib speech and social-context speech of Child J. The solid line denotes crib speech. The dashed line denotes social-context speech.

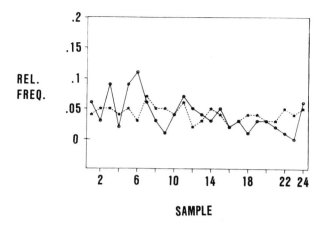

Figure 4-109. Across-sample comparisons of the relative frequency of exact reproductions in the crib speech and social-context speech of Child K. The solid line denotes crib speech. The dashed line denotes social-context speech.

M, and N). The two types of analyses yielded similar developmental patterns for social-context speech for 11 of the children (A, D, E, F, G, H, J, K, L, M, and N).

Summary of the Analyses of Developmental Patterns

The analyses just given, like the analyses presented before them, have demonstrated the extent of individual differences in the use of language practice in the two speech-sampling situations. However, there were nonetheless several general patterns:

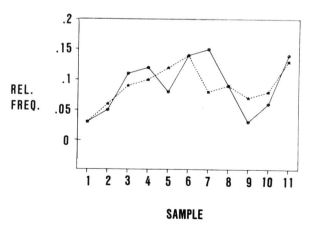

Figure 4-110. Across-sample comparisons of the relative frequency of exact reproductions in the crib speech and social-context speech of Child L. The solid line denotes crib speech. The dashed line denotes social-context speech.

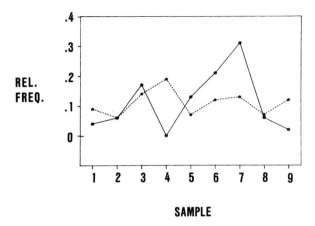

Figure 4-111. Across-sample comparisons of the relative frequency of exact reproductions in the crib speech and social-context speech of Child M. The solid line
denotes crib speech. The dashed line denotes social-context speech.

1. Buildups and substitutions tended to constitute a higher proportion of linguistic practice in crib speech than in social-context speech. Breakdowns tended to
comprise a higher proportion of linguistic practice in social-context speech than in
crib speech. The proportion of linguistic practice accounted for by completions and
exact reproductions was higher in crib speech for some children and in social-
context speech for other children (this being true for each of the two types of practice), with no discernable general pattern emerging in the data.

2. The within-sample comparisons were concerned with the extent to which lin-

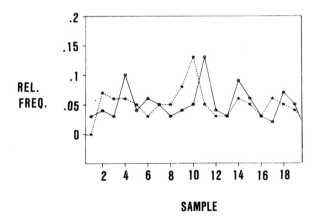

Figure 4-112. Across-sample comparisons of the relative frequency of exact reproductions in the crib speech and social-context speech of Child N. The solid line
denotes crib speech. The dashed line denotes social-context speech.

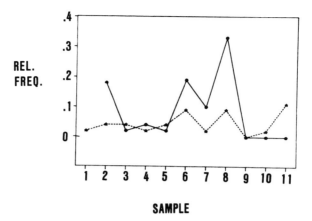

SAMPLE

Figure 4-113. Within-sample comparisons of the relative frequency of substitutions in the crib speech and social-context speech of Child A. The solid line denotes crib speech. The dashed line denotes social-context speech.

guistic practice consisted of each of the five target practice types, and how these proportions changed over time. In terms of these comparisons, the relative frequencies of buildups, completions, exact reproductions, and substitutions tended to be more variable in crib speech than in social-context speech. However, the relative frequencies of breakdowns were more variable in social-context speech than in crib speech.

The across-sample comparisons were concerned with the manner in which the frequency of use of a type of practice varied across samples. These comparisons

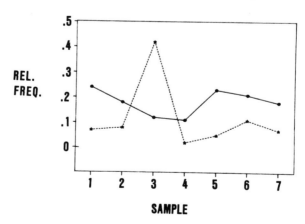

SAMPLE

Figure 4-114. Within-sample comparisons of the relative frequency of substitutions in the crib speech and social-context speech of Child B. The solid line denotes crib speech. The dashed line denotes social-context speech.

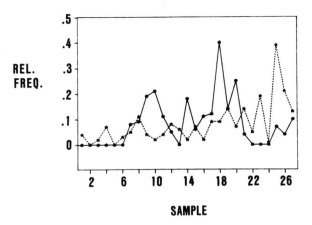

Figure 4-115. Within-sample comparisons of the relative frequency of substitutions in the crib speech and social-context speech of Child C. The solid line denotes crib speech. The dashed line denotes social-context speech.

revealed that the use of each type of practice tended to be more stable in social-context speech than in crib speech.

3. There were inverse relations in the relative frequencies of each practice type such that a peak in the relative frequency in social-context speech corresponded to a dip in the relative frequency in crib speech (and vice versa) for the same time period. This type of pattern was found for each type of practice in the within-sample comparisons, and for completions, exact reproductions, and substitutions in the across-sample comparisons.

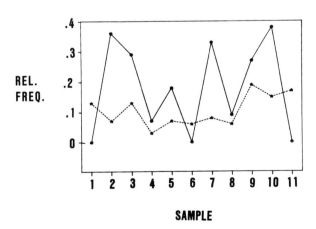

Figure 4-116. Within-sample comparisons of the relative frequency of substitutions in the crib speech and social-context speech of Child D. The solid line denotes crib speech. The dashed line denotes social-context speech.

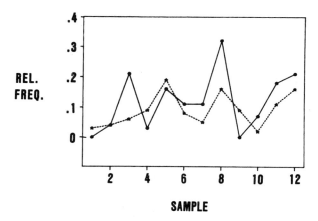

Figure 4-117. Within-sample comparisons of the relative frequency of substitutions in the crib speech and social-context speech of Child E. The solid line denotes crib speech. The dashed line denotes social-context speech.

4. There were few instances in which the developmental pattern revealed by either a within-sample or an across-sample comparison for a practice type paralleled that of MLU. Such parallel developmental patterns were most likely to occur in crib speech when they did occur. They were also more likely to occur for buildups and completions than for breakdowns, exact reproductions, and substitutions.

5. Peaks in the relative frequencies of each type of practice in crib speech tended to be associated with either a simultaneous increase in MLU in social-context speech or a subsequent increase in MLU in social-context speech. Crib-

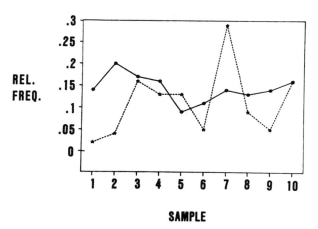

Figure 4-118. Within-sample comparisons of the relative frequency of substitutions in the crib speech and social-context speech of Child F. The solid line denotes crib speech. The dashed line denotes social-context speech.

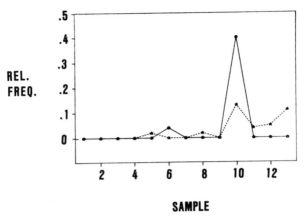

Figure 4-119. Within-sample comparisons of the relative frequency of substitutions in the crib speech and social-context speech of Child G. The solid line denotes crib speech. The dashed line denotes social-context speech.

speech practice, then, was related to the growth of productive grammatical skills in social-context speech.

6. The developmental analyses also revealed a few patterns in which a type of practice seemed to be learned (or its use consolidated) in one type of speech setting prior to its emergence (or more frequent use) in another speech setting. When this pattern was observed for buildups, it was invariably the case that crib speech was the setting in which the practice type was learned. However, the opposite pattern always held for breakdowns when one speech situation seemed to serve as a primary

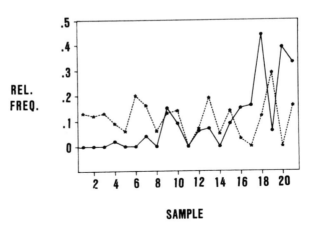

Figure 4-120. Within-sample comparisons of the relative frequency of substitutions in the crib speech and social-context speech of Child H. The solid line denotes crib speech. The dashed line denotes social-context speech.

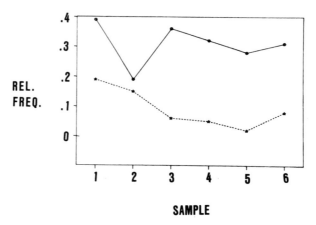

REL.
FREQ.

SAMPLE

Figure 4-121. Within-sample comparisons of the relative frequency of substitutions in the crib speech and social-context speech of Child I. The solid line denotes crib speech. The dashed line denotes social-context speech.

learning context for the practice type. For breakdowns, the social-context speech setting seemed to be the primary learning context. The use of completions was more likely to occur in social-context speech prior to crib speech. However, one child (A) exhibited the opposite pattern. The data do not suggest any systematic pattern in this regard for exact reproductions or substitutions. Some children seemed to learn to use exact reproductions or substitutions in social-context speech prior to doing so in crib speech; other children exhibited the opposite pattern.

7. The within-sample and across-sample comparisons yielded similar develop-

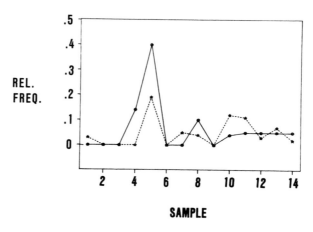

REL.
FREQ.

SAMPLE

Figure 4-122. Within-sample comparisons of the relative frequency of substitutions in the crib speech and social-context speech of Child J. The solid line denotes crib speech. The dashed line denotes social-context speech.

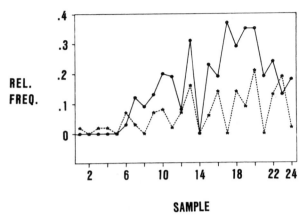

Figure 4-123. Within-sample comparisons of the relative frequency of substitutions in the crib speech and social-context speech of Child K. The solid line denotes crib speech. The dashed line denotes social-context speech.

mental patterns for each practice type in both crib speech and in social-context speech, but only for some children. In fact, in certain situations (e.g., breakdowns in social-context speech) similar developmental patterns in the two types of comparisons were less frequent than were different developmental patterns. Recall that the within-sample comparisons were concerned with the proportion of each type of practice in each speech sample. As such, these comparisons assessed the extent to which practice in each speech sample consisted of each of the five types of practice, and the extent to which these proportions varied from sample to sample. On

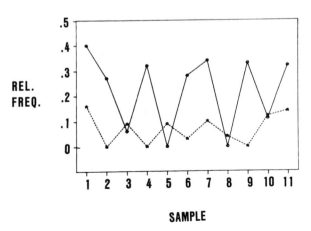

Figure 4-124. Within-sample comparisons of the relative frequency of substitutions in the crib speech and social-context speech of Child L. The solid line denotes crib speech. The dashed line denotes social-context speech.

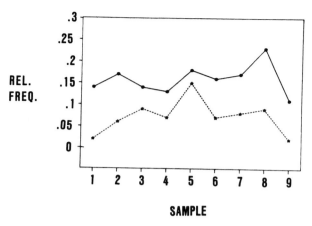

Figure 4-125. Within-sample comparisons of the relative frequency of substitutions in the crib speech and social-context speech of Child M. The solid line denotes crib speech. The dashed line denotes social-context speech.

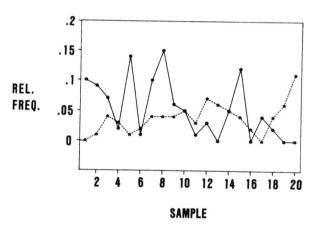

Figure 4-126. Within-sample comparisons of the relative frequency of substitutions in the crib speech and social-context speech of Child N. The solid line denotes crib speech. The dashed line denotes social-context speech.

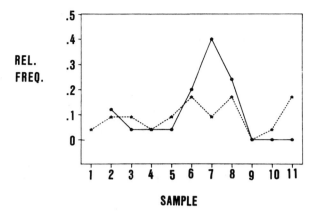

Figure 4-127. Across-sample comparisons of the relative frequency of substitutions in the crib speech and social-context speech of Child A. The solid line denotes crib speech. The dashed line denotes social-context speech.

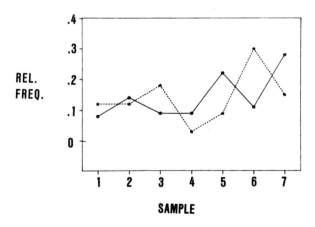

Figure 4-128. Across-sample comparisons of the relative frequency of substitutions in the crib speech and social-context speech of Child B. The solid line denotes crib speech. The dashed line denotes social-context speech.

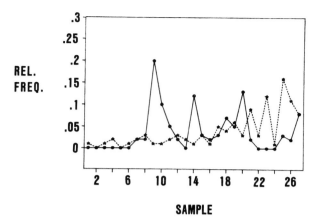

Figure 4-129. Across-sample comparisons of the relative frequency of substitutions in the crib speech and social-context speech of Child C. The solid line denotes crib speech. The dashed line denotes social-context speech.

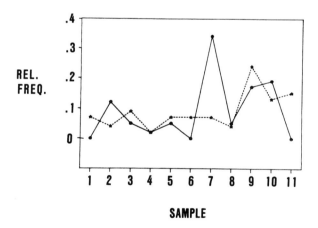

Figure 4-130. Across-sample comparisons of the relative frequency of substitutions in the crib speech and social-context speech of Child D. The solid line denotes crib speech. The dashed line denotes social-context speech.

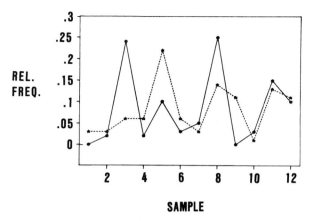

Figure 4-131. Across-sample comparisons of the relative frequency of substitutions in the crib speech and social-context speech of Child E. The solid line denotes crib speech. The dashed line denotes social-context speech.

the other hand, the across-sample comparisons revealed the extent to which each type of practice varied from speech sample to speech sample irrespective of the other four types of practice. Thus, when the two types of analyses revealed similar developmental patterns for a practice type for a child, the variation in the extent to which the practice type comprised the overall amount of language practice in a sample corresponded to the variation in the extent to which the practice type varied in absolute frequency from sample to sample. In order for similar developmental patterns to emerge in the two types of comparisons, the frequency with which a type

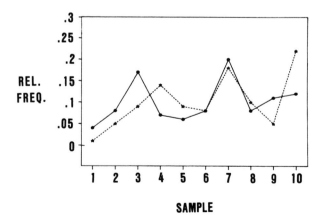

Figure 4-132. Across-sample comparisons of the relative frequency of substitutions in the crib speech and social-context speech of Child F. The solid line denotes crib speech. The dashed line denotes social-context speech.

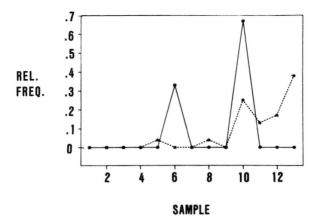

Figure 4-133. Across-sample comparisons of the relative frequency of substitutions in the crib speech and social-context speech of Child G. The solid line denotes crib speech. The dashed line denotes social-context speech.

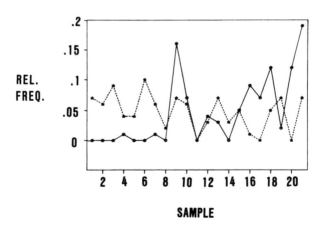

Figure 4-134. Across-sample comparisons of the relative frequency of substitutions in the crib speech and social-context speech of Child H. The solid line denotes crib speech. The dashed line denotes social-context speech.

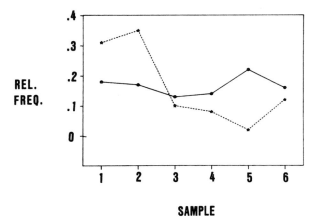

Figure 4-135. Across-sample comparisons of the relative frequency of substitutions in the crib speech and social-context speech of Child I. The solid line denotes crib speech. The dashed line denotes social-context speech.

of linguistic practice varied from sample to sample also affected in a similar fashion its proportion of overall linguistic practice. In other words, an increase (or decrease) in the absolute frequency of a practice type corresponded with an increase (or decrease) in the extent to which the practice type comprised the overall amount of linguistic practice in that sample. Given this, perhaps it is not surprising that there were many instances in which this relation did not hold. Still, the relation did hold in many instances, suggesting that in such cases the particular type of linguistic practice for which similar developmental patterns were found accounted for much

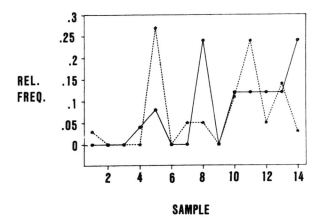

Figure 4-136. Across-sample comparisons of the relative frequency of substitutions in the crib speech and social-context speech of Child J. The solid line denotes crib speech. The dashed line denotes social-context speech.

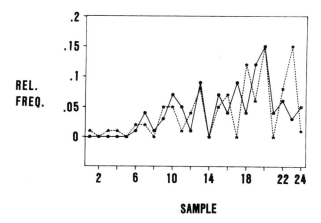

Figure 4-137. Across-sample comparisons of the relative frequency of substitutions in the crib speech and social-context speech of Child K. The solid line denotes crib speech. The dashed line denotes social-context speech.

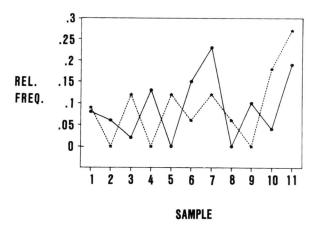

Figure 4-138. Across-sample comparisons of the relative frequency of substitutions in the crib speech and social-context speech of Child L. The solid line denotes crib speech. The dashed line denotes social-context speech.

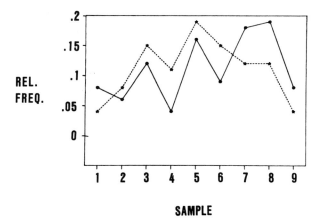

Figure 4-139. Across-sample comparisons of the relative frequency of substitutions in the crib speech and social-context speech of Child M. The solid line denotes crib speech. The dashed line denotes social-context speech.

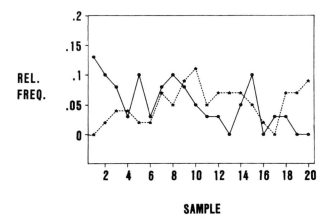

Figure 4-140. Across-sample comparisons of the relative frequency of substitutions in the crib speech and social-context speech of Child N. The solid line denotes crib speech. The dashed line denotes social-context speech.

of the variation in overall linguistic practice from sample to sample for that speech type. Such similarity was most likely to be found in social-context speech for buildups, completions, and substitutions, suggesting that these types of practice accounted for much of the variation in the frequency of language practice per se in social-context speech. In crib speech, buildups, breakdowns, and completions were the practice types most likely to exhibit similar developmental patterns in the two types of comparisons, suggesting that these types of practice accounted for much of the variability in language practice per se in crib speech.

5. Discussion, Conclusions, and Speculations

The data presented in Chapter 4 revealed a number of patterns regarding practice type, model type, and speech type. In the first part of this chapter, I shall summarize these findings. In terms of overall absolute frequency, exact reproductions were the most frequent type of practice, followed by breakdowns, buildups, substitutions, and completions (from most to least frequent). Practice was more frequent in social-context speech than in crib speech in terms of absolute frequency. However, practice comprised a larger proportion of the children's speech in the crib-speech samples than in the social-context-speech samples. Thus, although there were more instances of practice in social-context speech than in crib speech, a child-produced utterance was more likely to take the form of linguistic practice in crib speech than in social-context speech. Crib speech, then, seemed to be a context in which children were quite likely to engage in linguistic practice.

Practice was more frequent when the model utterance was produced by the child than when the model utterance was produced by another. There were four types of model contexts: (a) crib speech (a self-model situation), (b) social/other (an other-model situation), (c) asocial/self (a self-model situation), and (d) social/self (a self-model situation). Practice was most frequent in the crib-speech context, next most frequent in the social/other context, next most frequent in the social/self context, and least frequent in the asocial/self context.

There were also a number of significant interactions of practice type, model type, and speech type. Buildups, completions, and substitutions were most frequent in the crib-speech and the social/self contexts and least frequent in the asocial/self and social/other situations. Breakdowns were most frequent in the social/other and crib-speech situations and least frequent in the social/self and asocial/self situations.

Exact reproductions were most frequent in the social/other and the social/self situations and least frequent in the crib-speech and asocial/self contexts.

In both the crib-speech and social/self situations, exact reproductions were the most frequent form of practice, followed by buildups, substitutions, completions, and breakdowns (from most to least frequent). Exact reproductions were also the most frequent form of practice in the asocial/self situation, followed by substitutions, breakdowns, buildups, and completions (from most to least frequent). In the social/other situation, exact reproductions were the most frequent form of practice, followed by breakdowns, substitutions, buildups, and completions (from most to least frequent).

The above results are based on analyses of group data. The group data base was formed by combining the data from each of the 14 children. Analyses were also individually conducted on each child's speech samples. These analyses were intended to determine the extent to which the data from each child corresponded with the group data. Although there were considerable individual differences, there were a number of general findings. Buildups, completions, exact reproductions, and substitutions were more likely to follow a self-model than an other-model (one child exhibited the opposite pattern for substitutions). Eleven of the children were more likely to produce breakdowns following a model produced by another than following a self-model. The remaining three children exhibited the opposite pattern. These results once again illustrate the interaction of practice type and model type. These analyses also revealed the significance of crib speech as a context for linguistic practice, particularly insofar as practice based on self-models was concerned.

These results were supported by the analyses of the developmental patterns of practice use. These analyses revealed that buildups and substitutions comprised a higher proportion of linguistic practice in crib speech than in social-context speech, whereas breakdowns comprised a higher proportion of linguistic practice in social-context speech than in crib speech. No consistent pattern emerged for completions and exact reproductions in this regard. Some children were more likely to use these practice types in crib speech than in social-context speech, the opposite pattern holding for other children. The use of each type of practice tended to be more variable in crib speech than in social-context speech, both in terms of the relative frequency of the practice type compared to all practice and compared to the use of a particular practice type across samples. The one exception to this pattern occurred for breakdowns, and only in regard to the use of breakdowns compared to the use of practice per se. The analyses of developmental patterns also revealed numerous inverse relations in the relative frequencies of each practice type. These inverse relations involved a peak in the relative frequency of a practice type in crib speech and a corresponding dip in the relative frequency of a practice type in social-context speech (or vice versa).

The findings just given reflect general trends in the data suggested by both the analyses of the group data and the individual analyses of the data of each child. In spite of these general trends, there were numerous individual differences revealed by the data. Tables 5-1 and 5-2 summarize some of these individual differences. Even a casual perusal of these tables reveals both general developmental patterns and individual differences. These dual characteristics were present in virtually all of the analyses, as noted in Chapters 3 and 4, and so must be kept in mind when considering the implications of the data.

Despite the individual differences, all of the analyses have confirmed the importance of the type of model and the type of speech context for linguistic practice. Buildups, completions, exact reproductions, and substitutions were more likely to follow self-models than other-models, whereas breakdowns were more likely to follow other-models than self-models. As noted in Chapter 4, the children's linguistic competence (or lack thereof) can account for much of the interaction of practice type and model type. However, social variables and the nature of each type of practice also are likely to play important roles in regard to this interaction. Young children are unlikely to have a sufficiently rich productive linguistic competence to enable them to build up, complete, reproduce exactly, or substitute other forms in response to an utterance produced by an adult. That children ever build up an adult's preceding utterance, complete or exactly reproduce it, or substitute other forms while repeating part of the adult utterance most likely reflects the extent to which adults produce model utterances sufficiently simple (i.e., within the child's productive competence) to permit the child to engage in one of these activities. Adults do appear to engage in simpler and more consistent language behavior when

Table 5-1. Summary of Whether the Developmental Analyses Revealed Higher Relative Frequencies of a Practice Type in Crib Speech or in Social-Context Speech (in regard to the proportion of use of the practice type compared to the use of practice per se)

	Practice Type				
Child	Buildups	Breakdowns	Completions	Exact Reproductions	Substitutions
A	C[a]	C	[b]	S-C[c]	C
B	C	S-C	C	S-C	C
C	C	S-C	C		C
D		S-C	S-C	C	C
E		S-C	S-C	C	C
F	C	S-C	C	S-C	
G	C	S-C	S-C	C	C
H	C		C	S-C	
I		S-C	S-C		C
J		S-C	S-C	C	C
K	C	C		S-C	C
L	C	S-C	C	S-C	C
M	C	S-C	S-C	S-C	C
N		S-C	C		C

[a]C denotes higher relative frequency in crib speech.

[b]Blank space denotes no consistent difference between crib speech and social-context speech.

[c]S-C denotes higher relative frequency in social-context speech.

Table 5-2. Summary of Whether a Practice Type Appeared to be Learned First in Crib Speech or in Social-Context Speech

			Practice Type		
Child	Buildups	Breakdowns	Completions	Exact Reproductions	Substitutions
A	[a]		C[b]	S-C[c]	
B	C				
C	C		S-C	C	C
D	C		S-C		
E					
F					C
G		S-C	S-C		C
H			S-C		S-C
I		S-C			
J					
K					
L	C				
M				S-C	
N				C	C

[a]Blank space denotes that the practice type did not appear to be learned in one speech setting before another.

[b]C denotes crib speech.

[c]S-C denotes social-context speech.

speaking to young children (see Snow & Ferguson, 1977), but it is still the case that adults produce many utterances that are too difficult for young children to process and thereby engage in one of these four types of linguistic practice. Parents may differ in the extent to which they provide children with utterances that the children could build up, complete, repeat exactly, or respond to with a substitution. This in turn could result in individual differences in regard to the use of language practice and/or in regard to the acquisition of language. This possibility will be considered in more detail in a later section.

That adults rarely provide children with model utterances for children to build up is not surprising, for if we assume that a buildup reflects a child's productive competence, or even the upper limit of the child's productive competence in that the child can build upon the base provided by the earlier utterance (either self-produced or other-produced), the model for the buildup must be somewhat below this level of competence. Otherwise, the child simply cannot build upon the model. Adults rarely talk at the same level as young children, let alone below this level. Exact reproductions do not necessarily require a model below the upper limit of the child's productive competence, but the model must be within the child's productive limitations. Thus, it is not surprising to find that children are more likely to repeat exactly their own utterances than those produced by adults. Adults simply do not provide 1- and 2-year-old children with as many models to do so as do the children themselves.

Children were also more likely to complete their own utterances than to complete utterances provided by adults. This tendency most likely is due to both the children's linguistic competence and to social factors. Adults rarely produce sentences that children have the necessary linguistic competence to complete. Moreover, adults rarely allow children to complete their utterances. Adults do not provide children with many incomplete utterances that children could complete even if the children had the necessary competence. In fact, in the data provided by the 14 children and their parents, parents were much more likely to complete children's utterances than were children to complete parental utterances ($t(13) = 2.61, p < .05$).

It is somewhat more difficult to explain the children's tendency to substitute more frequently in their reproductions of their own model utterances than in their reproductions of utterances provided by others. This is no doubt partly due to the children's lack of linguistic competence relative to that reflected in the utterances produced by adults (even in the speech the adults are producing for the children). In order to engage in a substitution practice behavior, one must be able to reproduce most of the model utterance and substitute some form for those omitted in the reproduction. However, this does not account for the fact that the children were more likely to engage in exact reproductions than completions, regardless of whether the model utterance was provided by another or by the child. The capability to reproduce exactly a model utterance is not far removed from that necessary to engage in substitution practice. In an exact reproduction, one repeats the model precisely. A substitution requires deletion of an element (or elements) and the substitution of another element (or elements) in the original's place. This additional processing may partially account for the finding that substitutions are rarer in linguistic practice than are exact reproductions.

The Relation of Imitation and Repetition

Up to this point, I have summarized the findings of Chapter 4 and offered suggestions as to the possible reasons why certain patterns occurred. One of the major findings concerned the significance of the origin of the model—produced by the child or by a present other. Certain types of practice were more likely to occur following a self-produced model, other types of practice (most notably breakdowns) being more likely to occur following models produced by someone other than the child. This pattern has implications for the issue concerning the relation between imitation and repetition. Following the definitions provided in Chapter 1, imitation involves the reproduction of a model produced by another. Repetition involves the reproduction of a model produced by the self. The question of whether or not there was a relation between imitation and repetition was dealt with in the following manner: (a) Initially, the overall amount of practice involving self-models and the overall amount of practice involving other-models was determined for each child, self-models being considered as imitation and other-models being considered as repetition. (b) The average amount of imitation and repetition per week (combining crib speech and social-context speech) was determined for each child by dividing the number of imitations or repetitions by the number of weeks each child participated in the study. (c) These averages were then rank ordered and a Spearman rank order correlation coefficient determined for the rank orders. This analysis did not yield a significant correlation (r_s = .41). Thus, it was not the case that children who frequently engaged in imitation also frequently engaged in repetition. However, such a relation did hold for some children. Child F had the highest average amount of repetition per week and the second highest average amount of imitation per week. Child H had the second highest average amount of repetition per week, and the highest amount of imitation per week. On the other hand, Child G had the lowest average amount of repetition per week, but the fifth highest amount of imitation per week. Child J had the lowest average amount of imitation per sample, but the seventh highest average amount of repetition per week. Other than the positive relation between imitation and repetition for the two children most likely to engage in one of these types of practice, there was no consistent relation among children's use of imitation and repetition.

In order to determine the relation of imitation and repetition better, Spearman rank order correlation coefficients were also determined for each of the five types of practice. These analyses followed the same format as the one previously described, differing only in that each type of practice was considered individually. The correlation coefficients yielded by these analyses were not statistically significant insofar as breakdowns, completions, and exact reproductions were concerned. Children who were most (or least) likely to engage in these practice activities following a self-model were not necessarily most (or least) likely to do so when the model was produced by a present other. For example, Child A was the second most likely of the 14 children to produce a buildup following a self-model, but the least likely of the children to do so following an other-model. Child B was the most likely of the children to produce a completion following a self-model, but only the 11th most likely child to do so following an other-model. Child J was most likely of the children to exactly repeat herself, but the least likely to exactly repeat an other-model. In spite of this lack of consistency in general, there were individual instances of consistency. Child N was the most likely child to produce breakdowns following self-models and the most likely to do so following other-models. Child J was the least likely of the children to produce a completion following a self-model and only the 12th most likely to do so following an other-model. Child M was the least likely of the children to produce an exact reproduction following a self-model, and only the 13th most likely to repeat exactly an utterance produced by another.

The use of buildups following a self-model was positively related to the use of buildups following an other-model, r_s = .56, $p < .05$. The use of substitutions following self-models also proved to be related to the use of substitutions following other-models, r_s = .66, $p < .05$. Children who were more likely (or least likely) to use buildups or completions following self-models were also more likely (or least likely) to do so following other-models. There certainly was not perfect consistency in this regard. Child M was the fourth most likely of the children to produce a buildup following a self-model, but only the tenth most likely of the children to do so following an other-model. Child H was the most likely of the children to produce a substitution following an other-model, but only the eighth most likely to do so following a self-model. Nonetheless, there was far greater consistency between the use of practice type following a self-model and following an other-model for buildups and substitutions than for breakdowns, completions, or exact reproductions.

These results support earlier findings in regard to the extent of individual differences in imitation (Bloom et al., 1974). There are considerable individual differences in imitation. There are also considerable individual differences in repetition. Moreover, there are individual differences in the extent to which children's use of imitation predicts their use of repetition (or vice versa), these individual differences interacting with practice type to yield the above results. The data on which these analyses and conclusions are based are summarized in Table 5-3.

The Relation of Crib-Speech Practice and Social-Context-Speech Practice

In addition to the influence of the origin of the model on linguistic practice, the speech context proved to be an important variable in regard to the frequency of linguistic practice. In order to determine the nature of this relation better, Spearman rank order correlation coefficients were determined for linguistic practice in crib speech and in social-context speech. These correlation coefficients were determined using the same general procedures outlined in the preceding section. These analyses may be summarized as follows: (a) Practice in crib speech and practice in social-context speech proved to be positively correlated, $r_s = .78, p < .01$. Children who were most likely to engage in linguistic practice in crib speech were also most likely to do so in social-context speech. Children who were less likely to engage in practice in crib speech were also less likely to do so in social-context speech. (b) The use of completions in crib speech was positively related to the use of completions in social-context speech, $r_s = .64, p < .05$. This was also true for exact reproductions $(r_s = .74, p < .01)$ and for substitutions $(r_s = .66, p < .01)$. (c) The use of buildups and breakdowns in crib speech was not positively correlated with the use of these same practice types in social-context speech.

These findings mask certain individual differences in the data. Although in general the use of buildups and breakdowns in crib speech and in social-context speech were not related, certain children did exhibit similar patterns of usage. Child J was the 12th most likely of the children to produce buildups in both crib speech and social-context speech. Child N was the most likely child to produce breakdowns in crib speech and the second most likely to do so in social-context speech. As noted above, the use of completions, exact reproductions, substitutions, and overall practice in crib speech and in social-context speech were positively related. Nonetheless, certain children differed in their use of these practice types in crib speech and in

Table 5-3. Average Frequency of Each Practice Type per Week for Each Child

	Buildup		Breakdown		Practice Type Completion		Exact Reproduction		Substitution	
Child	S^a	O^b	S	O	S	O	S	O	S	O
A	15.5	2.6	11.5	5.1	20.0	0	20.9	4.4	4.2	.2
B	23.4	1.3	7.1	14.4	20.3	.1	26.9	8.3	13.3	.7
C	8.9	.8	1.0	9.6	1.9	.3	34.9	17.8	7.3	.4
D	5.7	.6	1.4	14.5	2.5	1.0	17.5	4.1	5.9	1.0
E	12.1	1.2	8.3	12.6	14.8	8.8	35.4	10.7	10.3	1.8
F	21.0	3.4	10.1	15.4	14.6	1.7	51.0	18.9	13.8	3.1
G	2.3	.2	2.3	23.8	.4	.2	16.3	9.8	1.8	.2
H	13.9	2.8	9.5	13.7	11.7	.1	57.9	18.9	6.5	8.3
I	15.3	.2	1.8	15.2	6.2	1.7	46.5	19.8	17.0	2.3
J	4.9	.3	3.9	6.1	.2	.1	62.1	2.5	3.5	.9
K	11.3	1.8	6.9	6.7	9.1	1.5	23.0	16.5	8.4	1.4
L	5.4	1.3	2.2	9.5	5.4	.9	19.1	13.7	6.4	1.0
M	19.3	.6	9.3	13.8	5.7	.4	13.1	3.9	7.4	1.1
N	21.1	1.9	18.0	26.5	13.3	0	16.9	12.5	4.6	.3

[a] S denotes practice based on a self-model.
[b] O denotes practice based on an other-model.

social-context speech. Child H was the third most likely of the children to use completions in crib speech but only the eleventh most likely to do so in social-context speech. Child H was the most likely of the children to produce exact reproductions in social-context speech, but only the fifth most likely to do so in crib speech. Child M was the sixth most likely of the children to use substitutions in crib speech, but only the eleventh most likely to do so in social-context speech. Child M was the eighth most likely of the children to use practice (all types combined) in crib speech, but the least likely to do so in social-context speech. The data on which these analyses are based are summarized in Table 5-4.

Once again, the general patterns revealed by the analyses are clouded by the individual differences revealed by the same analyses. Given that children differed from one another in terms of the extent to which their use of practice per se or their use of a practice type in one speech setting predicted their use of practice per se or a practice type in the other speech setting, and given that practice type interacted with these individual differences, it should be remembered that these general patterns reflect group tendencies rather than absolute predispositions on the part of each individual child.

It is also important to remember that the types of imitation-repetition do not appear independently of one another. Craig and Gallagher (1979) found that reduction-expansion-substitution combination repetitions increased with age. They also found that approximately 40% of children's reduction repetitions were preceded or followed by elaborations. This led them to speculate that reductions and elaborations "are essentially mirror images of the same basic linguistic principle" (p. 59). In their data, reductions and expansions seemed to occur in a parallel and reciprocal fashion. Thus, the "alternate addition and deletion of sentence elements is a primary linguistic analysis procedure for the young child" (p. 59). Craig and Gallagher also found that these repetitive *revision* sequences (reduction-expansion or expansion-reduction) occurred more frequently in monologue than in dialogue.

Parents' Modeling of Linguistic Practice

Parents frequently respond to children's utterance by imitating or modifying the utterance produced by the child (Cross, 1977; Kuczaj, 1982b; Slobin, 1968). Cross (1977) reported that children who were fast language learners had mothers who were more likely to provide an input of buildups, completions, and breakdowns (Cross called these expansions, extensions, and partial repetitions) than the mothers of children who acquired language in a less rapid fashion. This finding fits well with the notion that parents may facilitate children's language development by providing children with models of language learning strategies as well as with information about the structural, semantic, phonological, and pragmatic aspects of the language (Kuczaj, 1982b; Slobin, 1968). Although the consideration of the impact of parental modeling of practice types on children's acquisition of their mother tongue is beyond the scope of this volume, the consideration of the relation between children's and parents' use of practice types is not. If parents do influence chil-

Table 5-4. Average Frequency of Each Practice Type per Sample per Week for Each Child

	Practice Type									
	Buildup		Breakdown		Completion		Exact Reproduction		Substitution	
Child	C[a]	S-C[b]	C	S-C	C	S-C	C	S-C	C	S-C
A	10.8	8.0	6.8	10.8	7.7	13.5	5.7	21.5	2.3	2.3
B	16.3	8.4	3.4	18.1	11.6	6.4	12.3	22.6	9.3	4.7
C	4.5	5.1	.5	10.1	.7	1.6	14.9	37.6	2.2	5.4
D	1.8	5.4	.7	18.4	.4	3.8	8.6	14.7	3.7	5.0
E	3.2	10.1	3.6	17.3	7.2	15.2	17.3	28.8	4.9	7.3
F	15.0	9.4	8.9	16.6	10.6	5.7	18.5	51.4	18.5	35.6
G	1.4	1.1	1.2	24.8	.1	.4	7.4	18.7	.2	1.8
H	10.3	6.3	6.8	16.3	9.3	2.5	17.1	59.7	4.6	10.2
I	5.3	10.2	1.0	16.0	2.2	5.7	23.0	43.3	12.8	6.5
J	1.9	3.4	1.6	8.4	0	.3	31.4	33.1	1.8	2.6
K	9.2	4.0	5.6	7.9	4.0	6.6	7.8	31.7	6.3	3.5
L	4.2	2.5	1.7	10.0	2.6	3.6	5.9	26.9	4.4	3.0
M	14.2	5.7	7.2	15.9	1.8	4.3	5.8	11.2	5.7	2.9
N	10.4	13.8	9.1	23.8	5.3	4.3	15.1	34.8	2.1	3.0

[a] C denotes crib speech.

[b] S-C denotes social-context speech.

dren's practice behaviors, and if children's practice behaviors can be shown to influence their acquisition of their first language, then parents' influence on children's practice behaviors can be said to affect children's language development. The first step is to assess the relation of parental modeling of practice types and children's use of these practice types. It is this first step that will concern us here.

The initial analyses involved the comparison of parental and child use of practice. For overall practice (combining the five practice types) and for each of the practice types, parents and children were rank ordered in terms of the frequency of usage. The rank orders were determined by comparing the average frequency of practice or a practice type per sample in order to avoid problems caused by the variation in how long each child and his/her parents participated in the investigation. If parents do influence children's practice behavior, then we might expect high positive rank order correlations. However, the rank order correlations were not statistically significant for overall practice, completions, exact reproductions, or completions. Parent and child use of buildups and breakdowns did prove to be positively correlated ($r_s = .57, p < .05$ for buildups; $r_s = .63, p < .05$ for breakdowns). Thus, parents who are more likely to produce buildups and breakdowns are more likely to have children who engage in these practice types than are parents who are less likely to produce these types of practice. Although these findings do not demonstrate a cause-effect relation between parent and child use of a practice type, they do suggest that parents may influence their children's practice behavior, at least insofar as buildups and breakdowns are concerned.

Parents did differ from one another in terms of the frequency with which they provided models of each of the five practice types and in terms of the opportunities they provided children to engage in each of the types of practice when another has provided the model utterance. However, these differences among parents were not predictive of differences among the children. That is, the parents' modeling of practice types did not predict children's use of the practice types, except for the cases of buildups and breakdowns. Thus, the frequency with which parents expand (build up) or reduce (break down) their own or their children's utterances is reflected in the frequency with which children expand or reduce their own and/or others' utterances. However, the frequency with which parents complete utterances, exactly reproduce utterances, or substitute elements in reproduced utterances is not reflected in the frequency with which their children engage in these practice behaviors. The effect of parental modeling of the five practice types seems to be specific to those practice types that add or delete linguistic units (buildups and breakdowns, respectively). These types of practice seem quite likely to facilitate children's language development, particularly their grammatical development, and so even though parents do not seem to influence children's use of all practice types greatly they do seem to influence two important types of linguistic practice (see also Seitz and Stewart, 1975, and Folger and Chapman, 1978).

The preceding analyses and speculations have rested on the assumption that the influence of parental modeling of the five language practice types on children's language practice would be reflected in high positive rank order correlations of parental and child use of the practice types. Although the presence of such a relation is strong support for the notion that parental modeling of a practice type influences children's use of the practice type, the absence of a significant rank order correlation does not necessarily mean that parents do not influence their children's use of language practice in general or of particular types of language practice. Parents may simply need to provide children with some minimally sufficient amount of models of a practice type in order for the children to come to comprehend the significance of the practice type and so come to use it themselves. If so, parents may play an important role in children's use of language practice. This possibility is worthy of further investigation in that it bears directly on the issue of innate language-learning strategies versus learned language-learning strategies. If parents do, in any sense, teach children to use these five practice types, then it would appear that such language practice is learned. If parents do not affect children's language practice in any significant fashion, then such behavior may rest on innate language-learning capabilities (see Bowerman, 1974, Kuczaj, 1979, 1982b, Maratsos, 1979, and Slobin, 1973, for more detailed considerations of this matter). Of course, it is also possible that there is an interaction between innate predispositions and experience. In fact, this possibility is quite likely. Children may be predisposed to learn and use certain types of language practice, but their environment (i.e., the models of language practice types by adults and/or other children) may nonetheless influence the extent to which this predisposition is realized.

Why Do Children Engage in Language Practice?

In the preceding discussion, I have speculated that children may be predisposed to engage in language practice, and that the children's environment, most notably the types of models of language practice provided by others, may influence children's language practice. Why, though, do children engage in language practice? One answer assumes that children do so because such behavior helps them to learn their mother tongue (Cazden, 1976; Chao, 1951; Davison, 1974; deLaguna, 1927; Elkonin, 1971; Jespersen, 1922; Johnson, 1932; Kuczaj, 1982b; Stern & Stern, 1928). Another answer assumes that they do so because language play is intrinsically rewarding to children (Britton, 1970; Garvey, 1974, 1976; Kuczaj, 1982b; Lewis, 1936; Reynolds, 1976). These two answers are not mutually exclusive. Children might find language practice pleasurable and might also use it to facilitate their acquisition of their native language. In the following, I shall attempt to specify the manner in which language practice may help children to learn language.

Bowerman (1978) pointed out that language acquisition rests on two important interrelated phenomenon: (a) expansion of children's linguistic repertoire, and (b) reorganization of the linguistic knowledge that children have achieved. Bowerman used the term *reorganization* to refer to two types of analyses: (a) those analyses deeper than children's initial piecemeal or superficial ones, and (b) those analyses that involve the actual restructuring of previous analyses. She also noted that the dichotomy between unanalyzed forms and analyzed forms is misleading in that analysis is not an all-or-none phenomenon, but rather an ongoing process that eventually results in some fairly complete understanding of the material being learned (see also Bowerman, 1982a, 1982b). Language development, then, is best viewed as an ongoing process that involves continual analysis and reanalysis by children in their search for the distinctions that have organizational significance for the linguistic conceptual system (Kuczaj, 1982a; Maratsos & Chalkley, 1980).

The view of language development being advanced here accords well with the three modes of learning suggested by Rummelhart and Norman (1978). These modes of learning are (a) accretion, (b) tuning, and (c) restructuring. Accretion involves the accumulation of new information. Tuning involves changes in the categories and concepts the learner uses to interpret novel information. Restructuring involves the creation of new knowledge structures in order to better interpret new information and to impose a new organization on one's existing knowledge. According to Rummelhart and Norman, restructuring is a particularly important mode of learning in that it allows for new interpretations of knowledge, for different and (typically) improved accessibility to knowledge, and for changes in the manner in which one acquires new knowledge.

In the course of acquiring their mother tongue, children must continually acquire new knowledge (accretion), categorize this information (tune), and relate these categories to one another (restructure). In order to do this, children must be able to relate new bits of information with previously learned bits of information. The necessity of such comparisons for grammatical development is forcibly argued by Maratsos and Chalkley (1980).

> The essential information a child needs about a new relational term in order to predict appropriate grammatical usage is not the meaning of the term but at least one semantic-distributional pattern in which it can occur . . . . However, that is not the only analysis the child must make in order to build up this system. The child must be able to encode the semantic-distributional patterns and the connections among them which are a function of their application to overlapping sets of relational terms . . . . Encoding and representing the correspondence of the uses of terms in *different* patterns is crucial; the child cannot just analyze the individual patterns (p. 231; original authors' italics).

The argument, then, is that children must continually attend to, analyze, organize, and store for future comparisons the grammatical contexts in which an individual term has occurred. Children are not perfectly adept at doing this, and so development takes time and is filled with mistakes based on misanalysis. Nonetheless, comparisons of old and new information are critical for grammatical development. In fact, such comparisons are critical for *all* aspects of language development (and for all aspects of conceptual development, for that matter).

Children may use language practice to help them make the comparisons between old and new knowledge. If so, language practice may facilitate both the discovery of appropriate grammatical distinctions and the continual analysis of the grammatical system. In the following, I shall offer a speculative account of how language practice may function as a critical method for learning grammatical distinctions and for restructuring the developing grammatical system. I shall first consider practice based on models produced by present others.

It seems likely that many adult utterances, even those directed toward young children, are beyond the children's current level of linguistic competence. If so, then adult models that children use as the basis for subsequent linguistic practice may stretch children's productive capability and thereby provide the basis for the improvement of such capability. Even when children reproduce an adult model utterance exactly, the exact reproductions may have only been made possible by the presence of the model. That is, the model utterance may have provided the basis for the child's production of an utterance at the upper limit of his/her productive capability. So even exact imitations may facilitate language development in terms of providing children with models of utterances slightly beyond their spontaneous nonimitative productive capability.

Breakdowns based on other-models may facilitate language development in that children may realize the discrepancy between their reduced imitation and the model utterance. Children do not randomly imitate parts of model utterances, but instead consistently imitate the parts of model utterances that are either within or slightly beyond their current level of linguistic competence (Guillaume, 1926; Piaget, 1954; Preyer, 1882; Valentine, 1930). This apparently universal characteristic of reduced imitations suggests that children process more of the model utterance than they can reproduce, for otherwise we would expect reduced imitations to be more random than systematic, and such is not the case. Reduced imitations, then, are likely to be important for language learning in that children may process and store information about both the model utterance and their imitations of it, this information thus being available for subsequent analyses on the children's part.

Substitutions, completions, and buildups based on other-models all may assist the language learning child in the creation of linguistic structure, form classes, and rules. The model utterance produced by another provides the basis for a more complex utterance on the child's part when the child engages in either a buildup or a completion. In the process, children may learn more about the structure of their mother tongue. Substitution based on other-models may facilitate children's acquisition of language units and form classes by drawing children's attention to semantic-distributional characteristics and semantic-distributional similarities of individual words and bound morphemes.

Language practice based on self-models also seems likely to play an important role in children's acquisition of their first language. Children's exact repetition of their own utterances may serve to consolidate and/or restructure earlier acquisitions. Children's breakdowns of their own model utterances may help them to differentiate the components of sentences and thereby assist them in creating form classes and combinatorial rules. In building up their own models, children may be pushing their productive capabilities to their upper limits, perhaps significantly beyond that of their first turn productive capability. Buildups, then, may be a significant language-learning device in that they allow children to stretch their productive capability to its uppermost limits. Completions may serve a similar function. Children may be able to produce longer and more complex utterances by pausing and reorganizing their utterance plan than they are capable of producing in the absence of such pauses. The use of substitutions in practice based on self-models, like that based on other-models, may help children to learn form classes and their properties.

If these speculations prove true, then language practice based on other-models and language practice based on self-models may both serve important roles in the language-learning process. The main difference in the two types of practice concerns the source of the model utterance. In practice based on other-models, children must respond to information provided by others. In such instances, children have no control over the original utterance, but do have control over the manner in which they respond to the model utterance. In practice based on self-models, children have control over both the model utterance and the manner in which they react to the model. Thus, children have greater control in practice based on self-models than in practice based on other-models. Practice based on other-models may be beneficial to language-learning children in that the model utterance places constraints on children's responses that the children would not produce themselves. If children are able to respond to these constraints, then the result is likely to be some developmental advancement. However, if the model utterance produced by another is too far beyond children's competence, then the children will not be able to process the new information, the result being no contribution to developmental improvement of competence. In order for children to benefit from novel information, they must be able both to assimilate and accommodate the information in terms of their existing knowledge base. The novel information should be moderately discrepant (i.e., both novel and familiar) in order for optimal learning to occur (Kuczaj, 1982a; Nelson, 1978; Piaget, 1972). In practice based on other-models, another person has control over the information provided to the child, who must attempt to assimilate and accommodate the information provided by the model utterance. Whether or not the child is successful depends on the other person providing the appropriate sort of information. Thus, one might expect children to at least fail to learn much from many of the utterances provided by others, for the other-produced utterances may be too far beyond the children's competence for them to comprehend and resolve the discrepancy between the model utterance and their current understanding of the language system and its properties. The capability to respond to an other-model in terms of one of the five types of language practice would seem to indicate that the child has been able to process some sufficient amount of information from the model utterance in order for learning to occur (either accretion, tuning, or restructuring). Thus, practice based on other-models may facilitate language learning, even though not all utterances produced by others will provide the right combination of novel and familiar information to yield developmental improvement. Parents seem to differ from one another in terms of the opportunities they provide children to engage in language practice as well as in terms of how often they provide children with models of language practice (see earlier discussion). Some parents were quite likely to provide their children with opportunities to build up or complete a parent-produced utterance, other parents being much less likely to do so. This difference among parents could prove to be one that relates to individual differences among children in terms of language learning.

At any rate, practice based on other-models may serve to facilitate children's language development. This possibility also holds for practice based on self-models. Recall that practice based on other-models is most beneficial when the child is able to recognize and resolve a moderately discrepant event. This is also true for practice based on self-models, the difference being that the children establish the moderately discrepant events that they are to resolve. Control over a situation and its outcomes seems to be one of the aspects of play that children most enjoy (Britton, 1970; Lewis, 1936; Reynolds, 1976). One of the aspects of the situation that children may particularly enjoy controlling is that of establishing the moderately discrepant event and attempting to resolve it in a situation for which there is no external consequence for failure. This hypothesis gains support from the fact that children seem most likely to play with (practice) those things that they are in the process of acquiring (Britton, 1970; Piaget, 1962, 1966; Vygotsky, 1966). Kuczaj (1982b) summarized this view in the following manner:

> The basic assumption of this view is that by virtue of the control children enjoy in play situations, they become able to consolidate acquisitions which they are able to manipulate in the play situation . . . . The impact of playful manipulations of behaviors is thought to occur not only because of the degree of control children have in play situations, but also because the play situation is one in which children may freely simulate behavior. As such, children may create situations in which they can engage in activities in which the normal consequences of such activities are absent. Thus, children can experiment without worrying about normal consequences, but at the same time learn from the experience. Play, then, permits experimentation and feedback without the object world's interfering in the process. (p. 211)

Although this quote focused on play as a learning device for the child, the main points also hold for practice based on self-models, particularly for practice based on self-models in the context of crib speech and in social situations in which the child is not attempting to communicate with the present other(s) [the asocial/self situation]. However, the main point that I should like to emphasize here is that in practice based on self-models, children provide the learning opportunity by manipulating their own knowledge in systematic ways. Such practice should be most beneficial to children in that they provide themselves with both the opportunity and the means to resolve moderately discrepant events.

The argument, then, is that language practice based on other-models and language practice based on self-models help the young child to learn language. In the former, the child must be able to apprehend and resolve the discrepancy between the utterance produced by another and his/her own knowledge of language. In the latter, the child both establishes and resolves discrepancies. Both types of practice should facilitate grammatical development by virtue of allowing the child to experience the same item in different contexts and different items in similar contexts, such experience being essential for grammatical development (Maratsos, 1979; Maratsos & Chalkley, 1980).

Is Crib Speech an Important Context for Language Practice?

In the previous section, I have argued that buildups, breakdowns, completions, exact reproductions, and substitutions are important components of the language-learning process in that they assist children in the acquisition of grammatical distinctions, form classes, and combinatorial rules. I also argued that practice based on other-models and practice based on self-models are both important sources of learning, albeit for somewhat different reasons. In this section, I shall argue that crib speech is a particularly important context for language practice.

The crib-speech context is one in which children are free to engage in behaviors of their own choosing, without any normal external consequences. There are no other people present, and so children cannot fail in communication attempts, be corrected for inappropriate use of language forms, or scolded for using taboo words. In the crib-speech setting, children establish their own system of checks and balances, and only if they choose to do so. The crib-speech context, then, is perfectly analogous to the play setting in that real-world interference and consequences are either totally absent or at least minimized. Given that children seem to enjoy the mastery they experience in play situations, the crib-speech setting should be one in which language practice flourishes. Children have complete control in this setting, and may experiment freely. It should not be surprising, then, that children were more likely to engage in practice (in terms of relative frequency) in crib speech than in social-context speech.

In an earlier paper on the relative ease of acquisition of suffixes and prefixes (Kuczaj, 1979), I suggested that children process linguistic information at (at least) two levels: (a) the level of initial processing, which occurs in short-term memory shortly after children have been exposed to the input, and (b) the level of postinitial processing, which occurs at some later time when children are attempting to interpret, organize, and consolidate information that they have experienced over some longer period of time. Of the three modes of learning suggested by Rummelhart and Norman (1978), only accretion (the expansion of a child's linguistic repertoire) seems possible at the level of initial processing, and only then if this information is transferred to long-term memory. Both tuning and restructuring depend on postinitial processing, for both changing the categories and the concepts that are used to interpret novel information and the creation of new knowledge structures necessitates the comparison of new input and old knowledge. Thus, postinitial processing is a critical aspect of the language-learning process in that it is necessary for the gradual evolution of the arbitrary yet conventional linguistic conceptual system.

If postinitial processing is an important component of the language-learning process, and if the perception and resolution of moderate discrepant events is another important aspect of language acquisition, then crib speech may be an important learning context in that it provides children with the opportunity to engage in overt postinitial processing, as manifested by the five types of language practice, as well as other sorts of overt verbal behavior. This overt behavior may greatly help children to both comprehend and resolve moderately discrepant information, and thereby facilitate their language acquisition. The articulation of difficult material seems to make the material somewhat easier to process, even for highly verbal and intelligent adults, and so it seems reasonable to suppose that young children also benefit from articulating their postinitial processing of linguistic information. Crib speech may be a significant setting for language-learning children in that it provides them with total freedom to engage in overt practice behaviors that facilitate post-initial processing. In the crib-speech setting, other people are not available to in any way restrict the children's behavior. This aspect of crib speech may be the most critical, for it assures that children have the freedom to direct their own behavior.

The argument, then, is that children are most likely to notice discrepancies between their knowledge of language and linguistic input at the level of postinitial processing, and that crib speech is a context in which children may freely engage in overt behaviors that facilitate both postinitial processing and the successful resolution of moderately discrepant events. Although older children and adults may be able to notice discrepancies during the initial processing of linguistic information, it is unlikely that young children are able to do so. In addition to contributing to both tuning and restructuring, postinitial processing may also help children to learn to express earlier acquired meanings with newly acquired forms. The complementary hypotheses that new forms are first used to express old meanings and that new meanings are first expressed by old forms (Cassirer, 1955; Kuczaj, 1983; Werner & Kaplan, 1963; Slobin, 1973) may reflect differences between initial and postinitial processing. Children may initially store new forms and new meanings and later compare these new acquisitions with previous ones in postinitial processing. The assimilation of the new acquisitions with the old may result in the initial dominance of earlier acquisitions over newer ones, resulting in the developmental outcomes first suggested by Cassirer (1955).

Crib speech may also facilitate language acquisition in that the language practice and postinitial processing that occur in this context happen as children are preparing to sleep (or at least when their parents are hoping that the children will soon be ready to sleep). If sleep helps to consolidate knowledge acquisition, the accretion, tuning, and restructuring of knowledge that occurs during crib speech may be particularly important to language-learning children. This is admittedly highly speculative, but is a possibility worthy of further investigation.

Why Do Children Cease to Engage in Crib Speech and Language Practice?

One finding that was apparent at the outset of our analyses of the data was that children cease to use crib speech at an early age, typically before their third birthday (see also Weir, 1962). It is also true that children have greatly reduced their use of language practice by their fourth birthday (see Kuczaj, 1982b). Both of these developmental patterns most likely reflect two other developmental tendencies. First, as children get older, they have acquired more and more knowledge of their language, and so have less need to engage in practice. Second, practice and postinitial processing move from an overt level to a covert level with development (Kuczaj & Bean, 1982; Vygotsky, 1962). Behaviors that young children must vocalize in order to achieve success may be engaged in at the covert (or mental) level by older children and adults. Thus, the elimination of crib speech and the reduction of language practice by children does not necessarily imply that children have ceased to process and resolve discrepancies between new and old information. Instead, this activity has moved from an overt to a covert level.

Why, though, do children cease to use crib speech before they cease to use overt language practice in other contexts? There is no clear answer to this question. Perhaps children become more likely to wear themselves out during the day, and so are more likely to fall asleep. Or perhaps they learn to engage in subvocal behavior in bed in order to escape parental interference in their bedtime play activities. Or perhaps they simply cease to be interested in vocalizing in bed. The only thing that is certain is that the cessation of crib speech does not correspond to a cessation of overt language practice in social-context speech.

Language Practice As Connected Discourse

During the course of this volume, I have been referring to individual practice types, and may have given the reader the impression that these practice types occur in isolation. This is true on some occasions, but the more typical case is one in which children combine various types of language practice in what Weir (1962) referred to as *paragraphs*. Practice types, then, do not always exist as separate utterance sequences, but rather mixed together in a paragraph following a certain train of thought. This is particularly true in the uninterrupted and unprompted crib speech. In the following crib speech examples, notice not only the combination of practice types, but also how one utterance or set of utterances suggests the next, either by content or by form.

(1) He's in truck. (2) He's in back. (3) Miss Piggy in back. (4) I put Miss Piggy in back. (5) I put bunny rabbit in back. (6) I put Miss Piggy in trunk. (7) I put Miss Piggy in trunk first, first. (8) I put Miss Piggy in back. (9) Put bunny rabbit in the . . . back.

(1) Bebo go to bed. (2) ( ) go to bed. (3) You go to bed, you're bad. (4) I'm not bad. (5) You're nice. (6) Bebo. (7) Bad. (8) Go to bed. (9) Let's see ( ). (10) (Yatsee, yatsee) (11) I see your bed. (12) Is your bed. (13) Your bed. (14) Come here, Bebo. (15) ( ) your bed. (16) Here. (17) Go to sleep [2X].

The paragraphs constructed by the children have the nature of a chain complex (Vygotsky, 1962; Weir, 1962). Vygotsky defined the chain complex as "a dynamic, consecutive joining of individual links into a single chain, with meaning carried over from one link to the next" (1962, p. 64). Children's paragraphs tended to include linguistic exercises combined in a chain of semantic and syntactic connections, wherein each utterance provides either a semantic or a syntactic basis for the next. Nonetheless, the utterances in each paragraph do not progress logically to express a unified organized thought, but instead constitute a chain of single thoughts, each stimulated by the last and revolving around one general topic.

The five types of linguistic practice are particularly well-suited to this type of language play in that these forms supply a paradigm or formula within which children may easily experiment. In other words, the well-learned form provides freedom to experiment semantically and phonetically and allows for syntactic embellishments within a known framework (Weir, 1962). The paragraphs just given illustrate how these variations are carried out, and how the child may insert new vocabulary items and practice unfamiliar grammatical arrangements with ease (see also Craig & Gallagher, 1979).

Children in the process of acquiring language practice new forms using the various types of formulas previously discussed—buildups, breakdowns, substitutions, and completions, as well as exact reproductions. Whether they use particular types of practice in crib speech or social-context speech may depend on the opportunities that present themselves to use the new forms in either context. A greater than average amount of practice in crib speech may limit the necessity for practice in social speech. Or each context may act as a source of feedback and material for the other—new grammatical information or vocabulary is received in social speech, and then is practiced in crib speech, after which the child brings it into practice in the social context (Weir, 1962; Kuczaj, 1981). Or a new form may be practiced in social-context speech and further explored in crib speech.

Conclusion

The data presented in this volume have illustrated the interaction of speech context, practice type, and model type. I have suggested that these patterns may be significant in terms of the manner in which children use language practice to facilitate their acquisition of language. The accuracy of these hypotheses will be assessed in future analyses of the data. These analyses will relate the acquisition of particular linguistic forms to actual practice with the forms, and as such will allow the determination of exactly how practice influences acquisition.

Nonetheless, it seems likely that the specific aspects of language with which individual children play may depend on individual differences that also affect the processing and organization of linguistic information. Individual differences may prove to be the rule rather than the exception in language development (see Kuczaj, 1981, 1982a; Michell, 1982; Nelson, 1981). The following quote from Bowerman illustrates the importance of such differences:

> Some children may do a great deal of "in depth" linguistic processing, ferreting out hidden regularities, while others do less, getting along indefinitely with relatively unintegrated, superficial rules. In addition, children may differ with respect to the particular domains of language in which they discover regularities. Some patterns are no doubt recognized by virtually all children . . . while others are grasped by fewer. And finally, children, like adults, may differ along the dimension of linguistic caution/innovativeness, which means that failure to produce errors in a given domain may not unequivocally be taken as evidence that the underlying structured regularity has not been appreciated. (Bowerman, 1982a, p. 45)

Not only may children differ in terms of the manner in which they deal with linguistic information, but as revealed in the data presented in Chapter 4, they also differ in terms of the extent to which they engage in various types of linguistic practice. Children also differ from one another in terms of whether or not they engage in crib speech. It seems that most children do if given the opportunity, but certainly not all children do. Neither of my sons produced crib speech and yet both of them seemed to be normal language learners (Kuczaj, 1977, 1978, 1979, 1981; Kuczaj & Daly, 1979).

In closing, I should like to note that although I have liberally sprinkled terms such as *practice, analyze,* and *learn* in reference to the children's crib speech and language practice, this activity should not be perceived as dull and meaningless to the children. Linguistic practice in crib speech and in social-context speech is more than a method to learn. This behavior often serves the action in which the children are engaged, which often as not, is play. Language adds a valuable dimension to children's play, as well as being a resource for play in itself. The combination of play and language results in monologues and dialogues that are instructive and enjoyable to the child as well as charming and intriguing to those of us who study them.

References

Achenbach, T. *Research in developmental psychology: Concepts, strategies, and methods.* New York: The Free Press, 1978.

Black, R. Crib talk and mother-child interaction: A comparison of form and function. *Papers and Reports on Child Language Development,* 1979, *17,* 90–97.

Blank, M., Gessner, M., & Esposito, A. Language without communication: A case study. *Journal of Child Language,* 1979, *6,* 329–352.

Bloom, L. *Language development: Form and function in emerging grammars.* Cambridge, Mass.: M.I.T. Press, 1970.

Bloom, L., Hood, L., & Lightbown, P. Imitation in language development: If, when, and why. *Cognitive Psychology,* 1974, *6,* 380–420.

Bloom, L., Rocissano, L., & Hood, L. Adult-child discourse: Developmental interaction between information processing and linguistic knowledge. *Cognitive Psychology,* 1976, *8,* 521–552.

Bohn, W. First steps in verbal expression. *Pedagogical Seminary,* 1914, *21,* 578–595.

Bowerman, M. *Early syntactic development: A cross-linguistic study with special reference to Finnish.* Cambridge: Cambridge University Press, 1973.

Bowerman, M. Discussion summary—development of concepts underlying language. In R. Schiefelbusch & L. Lloyd (Eds.), *Language perspectives—Acquisition, retardation, and intervention.* Baltimore: University Park Press, 1974.

Bowerman, M. Words and sentences: Uniformity, individual variation, and shifts over time in patterns of acquisition. In F. Minifie & L. Lloyd (Eds.), *Communicative and cognitive abilities—Early behavioral assessment.* Baltimore: University Park Press, 1978.

Bowerman, M. Reorganizational processes in language development. In L. Gleitman & E. Wanner (Eds.), *The state of the art in language acquisition.* New York: Academic Press, 1982. (a)

Bowerman, M. Starting to talk worse: Clues to language acquisition from children's late speech errors. In S. Strauss (Ed.), *U-shaped behavioral growth.* New York: Academic Press, 1982. (b)

Braine, M. The acquisition of language in infant and child. In C. Reed (Ed.), *The learning of language.* New York: Appleton-Century-Crofts, 1971.

Braine, M. Length constraints, reduction rules, and holophrastic processes in children's word combinations. *Journal of Verbal Learning and Verbal Behavior,* 1974, *13,* 448–456.

Brainerd, C. *Piaget's theory of intelligence.* Englewood Cliffs, N.J.: Prentice-Hall, 1978.

Britton, J. *Language and learning.* London: Penguin Books, 1970.

Brown, R. The development of *wh* questions in child speech. *Journal of Verbal Learning and Verbal Behavior,* 1968, *7,* 277–290.

Brown, R. *A first language/The early stages.* Cambridge, Mass.: Harvard University Press, 1973.

Brown, R., & Bellugi, U. Three processes in the child's acquisition of syntax. *Harvard Educational Review,* 1964, *34,* 133–151.

Cassirrer, E. *The philosophy of symbolic forms* (Vol. 1). New Haven: Yale University Press, 1955.

Cazden, C. The acquisition of noun and verb inflections. *Child Development,* 1968, *39,* 433–448.

Cazden, C. Play with language and meta-linguistic awareness: One dimension of language experience. In J. Bruner, A. Jolly, & K. Sylva (Eds.), *Play—its role in development and evolution.* New York: Basic Books, 1976.

Chao, Y. The Cantian idiolect: An analyses of the Chinese spoken by a twenty-eight-month-old child. *Semitic and Oriental Studies,* 1951, *11,* 27–44.

Cherry, L. Role of adult requests for clarification. In R. Freedle (Ed.), *New directions in discourse processing* (Vol. II). Norwood, N.J.: Ablex Publishing Co., 1978.

Chomsky, N. Review of Skinner's *Verbal behavior. Language,* 1959, *3,* 26–58.

Chomsky, N. *Aspects of the theory of syntax.* Cambridge, Mass.: M.I.T. Press, 1965.

Chomsky, N. *Language and mind.* New York: Harcourt, Brace, Jovanovich, 1972.

Clark, E., & Anderson, E. Spontaneous repairs: Awareness in the processing of acquiring language. *Papers and Reports on Child Language Development,* 1979, *16,* 1–12.

Clark, R. Performing without competence. *Journal of Child Language,* 1974, *1,* 1–10.

Clark, R. Adult theories, child strategies, and their implications for the language teacher. In J. Allen & S. Corder (Eds.), *Edinburgh course in applied linguistics* (Vol. 2). London: Oxford University Press, 1975.

Clark, R. What's the use of imitation? *Journal of Child Language,* 1977, *4,* 341–358.

Clark, R. Some even simpler ways to talk. In N. Waterson & C. Snow (Eds.), *The development of communication.* London: Wiley, 1978.

Clark, R. Theory and method in child-language research: Are we assuming too much? In S. Kuczaj (Ed.), *Language development, Vol. 1: Syntax and Semantics.* Hillsdale, N.J.: Lawrence Erlbaum Associates, 1982.

Craig, H., & Gallagher, T. The structural characteristics of monologues in the speech of normal children: Syntactic nonconversational aspects. *Journal of Speech and Hearing Research,* 1979, *22,* 46–62.

Cross, T. Mother's speech adjustments: The contribution of selected child listener variables. In C. Snow & C. Ferguson (Eds.), *Talking to children: Language input and acquisition.* Cambridge: Cambridge University Press, 1977.

Davison, A. Linguistic play and language acquisition. *Papers and Reports on Child Language Development,* 1974, *8,* 179–187.

DeLaguna, G. *Speech: Its function and development.* Bloomington, Indiana: Indiana University Press, 1927.

Dore, J. Holophrases, speech acts and language universals. *Journal of Child Language,* 1975, *2,* 21–40.

Elkonin, D. Development of speech. In A. Zeporozhets & D. Elkonin (Eds.), *The psychology of preschool children.* Cambridge, Mass.: M.I.T. Press, 1971.

Ervin, S. Imitation and structural change in children's language. In E. Lenneberg (Ed.), *New directions in the study of language.* Cambridge, Mass.: M.I.T. Press, 1964.

Ferguson, C. Learning to pronounce: The earliest stages of phonological development in the child. *Papers and Reports on Child Language Development,* 1976, *11,* 1–27.

Ferrier, J. Some observations of error in context. In N. Waterson & C. Snow (Eds.), *The development of communication.* London: Wiley, 1978.

Fillmore, C. The case for case. In E. Bach & R. Harms (Eds.), *Universals in linguistic theory.* New York: Holt, Rinehart and Winston, 1968.

Flavell, J. *The developmental psychology of Jean Piaget.* New York: Van Nostrand Reinhold, 1963.

Folger, J., & Chapman, R. A pragmatic analysis of spontaneous imitations. *Journal of Child Language,* 1978, *5,* 25–38.

Fuson, K. The development of self-regulating aspects of speech: A review. In G. Zivon (Ed.), *The development of self-regulation through private speech.* New York: Wiley, 1979.

Gallagher, T. Revision behaviors in the speech of normal children developing language. *Journal of Speech and Hearing Research,* 1977, *20,* 303–318.

Gallagher, T., & Craig, H. The structural characteristics of monologues in the speech of normal children: Semantic and conversational aspects. *Journal of Speech and Hearing Research,* 1978, *21,* 179–199.

Garvey, C. Some properties of social play. *Merrill Palmer Quarterly,* 1974, *20,* 163–180.

Garvey, C. Some properties of social play. In J. Bruner, A. Jolly, & K. Sylva (Eds.), *Play: Its role in developmental evolution.* New York: Basic Books, 1976.

Garvey, C. *Play.* Cambridge, Mass.: Harvard University Press, 1977. (a)

Garvey, C. Play with language and speech. In S. Ervin-Tripp & R. Mitchel-Keenan (Eds.), *Child discourse.* New York: Academic Press, 1977. (b)

Gleitman, L. Maturational determinants of language growth. *Cognition,* in press.

Greenfield, P., & Smith, J. *The structure of communication in early language development.* New York: Academic Press, 1976.

Groos, K. *The play of man.* New York: D. Appleton and Co., 1901.

Guillaume, P. *Imitation in children.* Chicago: University of Chicago Press, 1926.

Hakuta, K. Prefabricated patterns and the emergence of structure in second language acquisition. *Language Learning,* 1974, *24,* 287–298.

Hiebert, E., & Cherry, L. Language play in young children's interactions with three co-participants. In D. Farkas, W. Jacobsen, & K. Todrys (Eds.), *Papers from the fourteenth regional meeting.* Chicago: Chicago Linguistic Society, 1978.

Hurlock, E. Experimental investigations of childhood play. *Psychological Bulletin,* 1934, *31,* 47–66.

Iwamura, S. *The verbal games of pre-school children.* London: Croom Helm, 1980.

Jakobson, R. *Child language, aphasia, and phonological universals.* The Hague: Mouton Publishers, 1968.

Jespersen, O. *Language: Its nature, development, and origin.* New York: Allen and Unwin, 1922.

Johnson, B. *Child psychology.* Baltimore, Maryland: Charles C Thomas, 1932.

Karmiloff-Smith, A. *A functional approach to child language.* Cambridge: The University Press, 1979.

Katz, J. *Semantic theory.* New York: Harper and Row, 1972.

Keenan, E. Conversational competence in children. *Journal of Child Language,* 1974, *1,* 163–183.

Keenan, E. Making it last: Repetition in children's discourse. In S. Ervin-Tripp & C. Mitchell-Kernan (Eds.), *Child discourse.* New York: Academic Press, 1977.

Keenan, E., & Klein, E. Coherency in children's discourse. *Journal of Psycholinguistic Research,* 1975, *4,* 365–380.

Keenan, E., Schieffelin, B., & Platt, M. Propositions across utterances and speakers. *Papers and Reports on Child Language Development,* 1976, *12,* 127–143.

Kleiman, A. *The use of private speech in young children and its relation to social speech.* Unpublished doctoral dissertation, University of Chicago, 1974.

Kuczaj, S. On the acquisition of a semantic system. *Journal of Verbal Learning and Verbal Behavior,* 1975, *14,* 340–358.

Kuczaj, S. Arguments against Hurford's "aux-copying" rule. *Journal of Child Language,* 1976, *3,* 423–428.

Kuczaj, S. The acquisition of regular and irregular past tense forms. *Journal of Verbal Learning and Verbal Behavior,* 1977, *16,* 589–600.

Kuczaj, S. Why do children fail to overgeneralize the progressive inflection? *Journal of Child Language,* 1978, *5,* 167–171.

Kuczaj, S. Evidence for a language learning strategy: On the relative ease of acquisition of prefixes and suffixes. *Child Development,* 1979, *50,* 1–13.

Kuczaj, S. More on children's initial failures to relate specific acquisitions. *Journal of Child Language,* 1981, *8,* 485–487.

Kuczaj, S. On the nature of syntactic development. In S. Kuczaj (Ed.), Language Development: *Syntax and Semantics.* Hillsdale, N.J.: Lawrence Erlbaum Associates, 1982. (a)

Kuczaj, S. Language play and language acquisition. In H. Reese (Ed.), *Advances in Child Development and Behavior.* New York: Academic Press, 1982. (b)

Kuczaj, S. Old and new forms, old and new meanings: The form-function hypotheses revisited. *First Language,* 1983, *3,* 55–61.

Kuczaj, S. *Deferred imitation and the acquisition of novel lexical items.* Unpublished manuscript, 1983, Southern Methodist University, Dallas, Texas.

Kuczaj, S., & Bean, A. The development of non-communicative speech systems. In S. Kuczaj (Ed.), *Language Development: Language, Thought and Culture.* Hillsdale, N.J.: Lawrence Erlbaum Associates, 1982.

Kuczaj, S., & Brannick, N. Children's use of the *wh* question modal auxiliary placement rule. *Journal of Experimental Child Psychology,* 1979, *28,* 43–67.

Kuczaj, S., & Daly, M. The development of hypothetical reference in the speech of young children. *Journal of Child Language,* 1979, *6,* 563–580.

Kuczaj, S., & Maratsos, M. What children *can* say before they *will. Merrill-Palmer Quarterly,* 1975, *21,* 89–112.

Kulikowski, S. Possible worlds semantics for early syntax. *Journal of Child Language,* 1981, *8,* 633–639.

Leech, G. *Semantics.* Baltimore: Penguin Books, 1974.

Leonard, L., & Kaplan, L. A note on imitation and lexical acquisition. *Journal of Child Language,* 1976, *3,* 449–456.

Leopold, W. *Speech development of a bilingual child.* Evanston, Ill.: Northwestern University Press, 1949.

Lewis, M. *Infant speech.* London: Routledge and Kegan Paul, 1936.

Lyons, J. *Semantics.* Cambridge: University Press, 1977.

MacWhinney, B. Rules, rote, and analogy in morphological formations by Hungarian children. *Journal of Child Language,* 1975, *2,* 65–77.

MacWhinney, B. Hungarian research on the acquisition of morphology and syntax. *Journal of Child Language,* 1976, *3,* 397–410.

MacWhinney, B. The acquisition of morphophonology. *Monographs of the Society for Research in Child Development,* 1978, *43,* (Nos. 1–2).

MacWhinney, B. Basic syntactic processes. In S. Kuczaj (Ed.), *Language development: Vol. 1, syntax and semantics.* Hillsdale, N.J.: Lawrence Erlbaum Associates, 1982.

Maratsos, M. How to get from words to sentences. In D. Aaronson & R. Rieber (Eds.), *Psycholinguistic research: Implications and applications.* Hillsdale, N.J.: Lawrence Erlbaum Associates, 1979.

Maratsos, M. Some current issues in the study of the acquisition of grammar. In P. Mussen (Ed.), *Carmichael's manual of child psychology.* New York: Wiley, in press.

Maratsos, M., & Chalkley, M. The internal language of children's syntax: The ontogenesis and representation of syntactic categories. In K. Nelson (Ed.), *Children's language* (Vol. II). New York: Gardner Press, 1980.

Maratsos, M., Kuczaj, S., Fox, D., & Chalkley, M. Some empirical findings in the acquisition of transformational relations: Passives, negatives, and the past tense. In W. A. Collins (Ed.), *Children's language and communication, The Minnesota Symposium on Child Psychology* (Vol. 12). Hillsdale, N.J.: Lawrence Erlbaum Associates, 1979.

Martlew, M., Connolly, K., & McCleod, C. Language use, rule and context in a five-year-old. *Journal of Child Language,* 1978, *5,* 81–99.

McNeill, D. *The acquisition of language: The study of developmental psycholinguistics.* New York: Harper and Row, 1970.

McTear, M. *Repairs: Learning to do it yourself.* Paper presented at the 2nd International Congress for the Study of Child Language, Vancouver, Canada, August, 1981.

Menyuk, P. A preliminary evaluation of grammatical capacity in children. *Journal of Verbal Learning and Verbal Behavior,* 1963, *2,* 429–439.

Michell, L. Language styles of 10 nursery school children. *First Language,* 1982, *3,* 1–28.

Miller, M. *The logic of language development in early childhood.* New York: Springer-Verlag, 1979.

Moerk, E. Processes and products of imitation: Evidence that imitation is progressive. *Journal of Psycholinguistic Research,* 1977, *6,* 187–202.

Nelson, K. Individual differences in language development: Implications for development and language. *Developmental Psychology,* 1981, *17,* 170–187.

Nelson, K. E. *Toward a rare-event cognitive comparison theory of syntax acquisition.* Paper presented at the 1st International Congress for the Study of Child Language, Tokyo, August, 1978.

Patrick, G. The psychology of play. *Pedagogical Seminary,* 1914, *21,* 469–484.

Piaget, J. *The children's conception of the world.* New York: Harcourt and Brace, 1929.

Piaget, J. *Play, dreams, and imitation in childhood.* New York: Norton, 1951.

Piaget, J. Language and thought from the genetic point of view. *Acta Psychologic,* 1954, *10,* 51–60.

Piaget, J. *The language and thought of the child.* Cleveland: Meridian, 1955.

Piaget, J. Comments on Vygotsky's critical remarks concerning *The language and thought of the child,* and *Judgment and reasoning in the child.* In L. S. Vygotsky, *Thought and language.* Cambridge, Mass.: M.I.T. Press, 1962.

Piaget, J. *The origins of intelligence in children.* New York: Norton, 1963.

Piaget, J. *Psychology of intelligence.* Totawa, N.J.: Littlefield, Adams, and Co., 1966.

Pickert, S. Imaginative dialogues in children's private speech. *First Language,* 1981, *2,* 5–20.

Preyer, W. *Die Seele des Kindes.* Leipzig: Grieben, 1882.

Ramer, A. The function of imitation in child language. *Journal of Speech and Hearing Research,* 1976, *19,* 700–717.

Reilly, J. *Children's repairs.* Paper presented at the 2nd International Congress for the Study of Child Language, Vancouver, Canada, August, 1981.

Reynolds, P. Play, language, and human evolution. In J. Bruner, A. Jolly, & K. Sylva (Eds.), *Play: Its role in development and evolution.* New York: Basic Books, 1976.

Rodd, L., & Braine, M. Children's imitations of syntactic constructions as a measure of linguistic competence. *Journal of Verbal Learning and Verbal Behavior,* 1970, *10,* 430–441.

Rodgon, M., & Kurdek, L. Vocal and gestural imitation in children under two years old. *Journal of Genetic Psychology,* 1977, *131,* 115–123.

Rogers, S. Self-initiated corrections in the speech of infant school children. *Journal of Child Language,* 1978, *5,* 365–371.

Rubin, K. The impact of the natural setting on private speech. In G. Zivin (Ed.), *The development of self-regulation through private speech.* New York: Wiley, 1979.

Rubin, K., Hultsch, D., & Peters, D. Non-social speech in four-year-old children as a function of birth order and interpersonal situation. *Merrill-Palmer Quarterly,* 1971, *17,* 41–50.

Rummelhart, D., & Norman, D. Accretion, tuning, and restructuring: Three modes of learning. In J. Cotton & R. Klatzky (Eds.), *Semantic factors in cognition.* Hillsdale, N.J.: Lawrence Elbaum Associates, 1978.

Ryan, J. Interpretation and imitation in early language development. In R. Hinde & J. Stevenson-Hinde (Eds.), *Constraints on learning.* New York: Academic Press, 1973.

Sadock, J. *Towards a linguistic theory of speech acts.* New York: Academic Press, 1974.

Savic, S. *How twins learn to talk.* New York: Academic Press, 1980.

Scollon, R. *Conversations with a one-year-old.* Honolulu: University Press of Hawaii, 1976.

Scollon, R. A real early stage: An unzippered condensation of a dissertation on child language. In E. Ochs & B. Schieffelin (Eds.), *Developmental pragmatics.* New York: Academic Press, 1979.

Searle, J. *Speech acts.* Cambridge: Cambridge University Press, 1969.

Seitz, S., & Stewart, C. Expanding on expansions and related aspects of mother-child communication. *Developmental Psychology,* 1975, *11,* 763–768.

Shields, M. Dialogue, monologue and egocentric speech by children in nursery schools. In O. Garnica & M. King (Eds.), *Language, children and society.* Oxford: Pergamon, 1979.

Shipley, E., Smith, C., and Gleitman, L. A study in the acquisition of language: Free responses to commands. *Language,* 1969, *45,* 322–342.

Skinner, B. *Verbal behavior.* New York: Appleton-Century-Crofts, 1957.

Slobin, D. Imitation and grammatical development in children. In E. Endler, L. Boulter, & H. Osser (Eds.), *Contemporary issues in developmental psychology.* New York: Holt, 1968.

Slobin, D. Cognitive prerequisites for the acquisition of grammar. In C. Ferguson and D. Slobin (Eds.), *Studies of child language development.* New York: Holt, Rinehart and Winston, 1973.

Snow, C. The uses of imitation. *Journal of Child Language,* 1981, *8,* 205–212.

Snow, C., & Ferguson, C. *Talking to children.* New York: Cambridge University Press, 1977.

Snyder, A. Notes on the talk of a two-and-a-half year old boy. *Pedagogical Seminary,* 1914, *21,* 412–424.

Stern, C., & Stern, W. *Die Kindersprache.* Leipzig, 1928.

Valentine, C. The psychology of imitation with special reference to early childhood. *British Journal of Psychology,* 1930, *21,* 105–132.

Valentine, C. *The psychology of early childhood.* London: Methuen, 1942.

Vinacke, W. E. *The psychology of thinking.* New York: McGraw-Hill, 1974.

Vygotsky, L. S. *Thought and language.* Cambridge, Mass.: M.I.T. Press, 1962.

Vygotsky, L. S. Play and its role in the mental development of the child. *Soviet Psychology,* 1966, *12,* 62–76.

Weeks, T. E. *Born to talk.* Rowley, Mass.: Newbury, 1979.

Weir, R. H. *Language in the crib.* The Hague: Mouton, 1962.

Werner, H., & Kaplan, B. *Symbol formation.* New York: Wiley, 1963.

Wexler, K., and Culicover, P. *Formal principles of language acquisition.* Cambridge, Mass.: M.I.T. Press, 1980.

Zakharova, A. Acquisition of forms of grammatical case by preschool children. In C. Ferguson & D. Slobin (Eds.), *Studies of child language development.* New York: Holt, Rinehart and Winston, 1973.

Zivin, G. Removing common confusions about egocentric speech, private speech and self-regulation. In G. Zivin (Ed.), *The development of self-regulation through private speech.* New York: Wiley, 1979.

Author Index

Achenbach, T., 8, 171
Anderson, E., 17, 172

Bean, A., 9, 168, 174
Bellugi, U., 5, 15, 172
Black, R., 12, 171
Blank, M., 16, 171
Bloom, L., 5, 11, 171
Bohn, W., 5, 11, 171
Bowerman, M., 5, 7, 162, 170, 171
Braine, M., 3, 5, 8, 16, 17, 18, 171, 172, 176
Brainerd, C., 1, 172
Brannick, N., 2, 174
Britton, J., 5, 7, 8, 11, 12, 13, 162, 166, 172
Brown, R., 5, 7, 15, 16, 24, 25, 172

Cassirrer, E., 168, 172
Cazden, C., 14, 16, 162, 172
Chalkley, M., 2, 12, 16, 163, 166, 175
Chao, Y., 14, 162, 172
Chapman, R., 6, 161, 173
Cherry, L., 15, 17, 172
Chomsky, N., 1, 2, 172

Clark, E., 17, 172
Clark, R., 15, 16, 172
Connolly, K., 10, 15, 175
Craig, H., 8, 10, 11, 159, 170, 172
Cross, T., 159, 172
Culicover, P., 1, 177

Daly, M., 171, 174
Davison, A., 14, 162, 173
deLaguna, G., 14, 162, 173
Dore, J., 5, 173

Elkonin, D., 14, 162, 173
Ervin, S., 5, 173
Esposito, A., 16, 171

Ferguson, C., 16, 154, 173
Ferrier, J., 16, 173
Fillmore, C., 1, 173
Flavell, J., 1, 173
Folger, J., 6, 161, 173
Fox, D., 12, 175
Fuson, K., 9, 10, 173

Gallagher, T., 8, 10, 11, 17, 159, 170, 173

Garvey, C., 3, 8, 9, 10, 11, 13, 24, 162, 173
Gessner, M., 16, 171
Gleitman, L., 7, 8, 173
Greenfield, P., 18, 173
Groos, K., 8, 173
Guillaume, P., 8, 164, 173

Hakuta, K., 16, 173
Hiebert, E., 15, 173
Hood, L., 7, 15, 18, 41, 157, 171
Hultsch, D., 10, 176
Hurlock, E., 5, 8, 173

Iwamura, S., 5, 17, 174

Jakobson, R., 1, 174
Jesperson, O., 11, 12, 14, 162, 174
Johnson, B., 5, 11, 14, 162, 174

Kaplan, B., 168, 177
Kaplan, L., 15, 175
Karmiloff-Smith, A., 17, 174
Katz, J., 1, 174
Keenan, E., 5, 10, 13, 18, 174
Kleiman, A., 11, 174
Klein, E., 10, 13, 174
Kuczaj, S., 2, 3, 4, 5, 6, 7, 8, 9, 12, 13, 14, 15, 16, 18, 23, 38, 159, 162, 163, 165, 166, 167, 168, 170, 171, 174, 175
Kulikowski, S., 3, 175
Kurdek, L., 7, 176

Leech, G., 1, 175
Leonard, L., 15, 175
Leopold, W., 8, 17, 175
Lewis, M., 8, 13, 162, 166, 175
Lightbown, P., 7, 15, 41, 157, 171
Lyons, J., 1, 175

MacWhinney, B., 15, 175
Maratsos, M., 1, 2, 8, 12, 16, 18, 162, 163, 166, 174, 175
Martlew, M., 10, 15, 175
McCleod, C., 10, 15, 175
McNeill, D., 2, 175
McTear, M., 17, 175
Menyuk, P., 5, 175

Michell, L., 170, 175
Miller, M., 5, 7, 175
Moerk, E., 7, 175

Nelson, K., 170, 175
Nelson, K.E., 2, 165, 176
Norman, D., 163, 167, 176

Patrick, G., 13, 176
Peters, D., 10, 176
Piaget, J., 2, 5, 8, 9, 10, 12, 13, 14, 15, 24, 164, 165, 166, 176
Pickert, S., 5, 12, 176
Platt, M., 18, 174
Preyer, W., 8, 164, 176

Ramer, A., 7, 176
Reilly, J., 17, 18, 176
Reynolds, P., 13, 162, 166, 176
Rocissano, L., 18, 171
Rodd, L., 5, 176
Rodgon, M., 7, 176
Rogers, S., 17, 176
Rubin, K., 5, 10, 176
Rummelhart, D., 163, 167, 176
Ryan, J., 7, 14, 15, 176

Sadock, J., 1, 176
Savic, S., 17, 176
Schieffelin, B., 18, 174
Scollon, R., 5, 8, 16, 18, 177
Searle, J., 1, 177
Seitz, S., 6, 161, 177
Shields, M., 11, 177
Shipley, E., 7, 177
Skinner, B., 2, 177
Slobin, D., 2, 5, 6, 7, 159, 162, 168, 177
Smith, C., 7, 177
Smith, J., 18, 173
Snow, C., 7, 15, 154, 177
Snyder, A., 3, 8, 11, 17, 177
Stern, C., 8, 14, 162, 177
Stern, W., 8, 14, 162, 177
Stewart, C., 6, 161, 177

Valentine, C., 5, 7, 8, 164, 177
Vinacke, W.E., 13, 177
Vygotsky, L.S., 9, 13, 166, 168, 169, 177

Weeks, T.E., 8, 177
Weir, R.H., 3, 5, 8, 10, 11, 12, 16, 17,
    168, 169, 170, 177
Werner, H., 168, 177

Wexler, K., 1, 177

Zakharova, A., 17, 177
Zivin, G., 10, 177

Subject Index

Abstract form classes, *see* Form classes
Accretion, 163, 165, 167
Across-sample comparison, *see* Development
Alliteration, 8
Analyses, 39, 162
  group, 37–43 *see also* Comparisons, Development
Appropriate learning climate, 122
  see also Environment, Social setting
Asocial speech, 19, 77
  see also Speech
Assimilation, 13, 165, 168
Auxiliaries, 26

Behavior, 8–9, 12–13, 159, 161, 167–168, 171
  covert, 2
  overt, 2–3, 167–168
  practice, 41, 161
  subvocal, 169
  verbal, 167
Breakdowns, 3–4, 19, 37, 39–77, 151–161, 164, 166, 170
  see also Development patterns

Categories, 167
Catentatives, 26
Chain complex, 169
Codable discrepancies, 2, 17
Cognitive skills, 1–2
  growth, 2
Communication, 3, 9, 24, 38, 41, 61–62, 66–67, 72, 105, 166–167
Comparisons, group, 26, 126, 136
  see also Analyses
Competence, 13, 16–19, 42, 153–155, 163–165
  see also Production
Completions, 3–4, 19, 37, 40–77, 151–161, 164, 166, 170
  see also Development
Complex utterances, 18, 164
Comprehension, 1, 162
Concepts, 167
Conceptual system, 1, 163, 167
Consolidation, 105, 164, 167–168
Context, 2–3, 50, 166, 168
Conventions, 9
Covert level, 168

Crib speech, definition of, 11–13
  see also Monologue, Nonsocial speech

Development, 1, 7
  breakdowns, across sample, 99–103
  breakdowns, within sample, 94–99
  breakdowns, within and across sample,
    103
  build-ups, across sample, 86–94
  build-ups, within sample, 78–85
  build-ups, within and across sample, 93
  completions, across sample, 109–114
  completions, within sample, 104–109
  completions, within and across sample,
    114–115
  conceptual, 163
  exact reproductions, across sample, 121–
    125
  exact reproductions, within sample, 115–
    121
  exact reproductions, within and across
    sample, 125–126
  patterns, 5–8, 14, 78
  substitutions, across sample, 130–133
  substitutions, within sample, 126–130
  substitutions, within and across sample,
    133–134
  tendencies, 78
  see also Grammatical development

Environment, 1–3, 8, 162
  mother-present, 10
Evolution, 167
Expansions, 18, 161
  parental, 6
  see also Imitation, Repetition, Repro-
    duction
Experience, 2, 14, 162, 166

Form classes, 2, 14, 164, 167
  abstract, 1–2

Grammatical, development, 6–7, 15, 25,
    35, 42, 84–85, 93, 114, 125, 130,
    133, 161, 163, 166, 170
  distinction, 163, 167
  skills, 139
  system, 11, 163
  utterances, 5

  see also Modifications
Group analyses, *see* Analyses
Group trends, *see* Trends

Imitation, 3–10
  delayed, 15
  exact, 4–5, 7
  expanded, 4–5, 7
  partial, 50
  reduced, 4–5, 7
  spontaneous, 5, 7
Individual differences, 5, 7, 15, 19, 26,
    34–35, 41, 44, 49, 77, 134, 152–154,
    157, 159, 165, 170
Initial processing, 167
Innate, 3, 162
  see also Predisposition
Input, 2, 16, 168
Intake, 2
Internal contexts, 2
Internal structure, 16
Intrinsic motivation, 2
Inverse relation, 26–29, 31, 33–34, 82–83,
    89–90, 96, 101, 108, 111, 118, 123–
    124, 131, 137, 152

Language-learning strategies, 81, 159
Lexicon, 1, 14

Mean length of utterance (MLU), 7, 10,
    19, 24–35, 78, 82–85, 93, 97–99,
    102, 108–109, 112, 114, 119–121,
    124–125, 129–130, 132–133, 138
Memorization, 16
Memory, 46
  long term, 167
  short term, 167
Methodology, 21–24
  scoring, 23–24
  subjects, 21–22
  transcription, 23
Model utterances, *see* Utterances
Modification, 3–5, 8–9, 11, 17
  grammatical, 10
Monologue, speech, 10, 24, 159, 171
  presleep, 11
  see also Crib speech
Morpheme, 12
  bound, 164

constituent, 25
see also Mean length of utterance

New forms, 168
Noncommunicative speech, 64, 67, 72, 76
Nonsocial speech, 10
see also Monologue, Private speech

Old forms, 168
Ongoing process, 162
see also Development
Overt speech, 12
level, 168–169
rehearsal, 15

Paragraphs, 11, 169
Patterns, 42, 67, 95, 118, 138, 151, 155,
157, 170
consistent, 88, 152
general, 49, 77, 134–144, 159
individual, 43
opposite, 52, 61, 63, 71, 77, 81, 92,
96, 104, 116, 118, 128, 139–140,
152
systematic, 139
see also Development
Perception, 167
Phonology, 1, 12–13, 17, 159, 169
Play, word, 10
see also Social, Social-context, Solitary
play
Pragmatic, 159
Post-initial processing, 167–168
Predisposition, 62, 77, 159, 162
see also Innate
Prefabricated, patterns, 16
routines, 16
Prefixes, 167
Production, 1, 12, 16, 19, 46, 125, 153–
154, 164
limitation, 154

Rank order, 77–78, 161
see also Spearman
Reduce, 161
see also Development
Rehearsal, *see* Behavior
Reorganization, 162
Repairs, 17–18

see also Spontaneous repairs
Repetition, 3–8, 155–157
exact, 19
expanded, 5
reduced, 5, 159
self, 5, 8
Replacement sequence, 16
Reproduction, exact, 4–5, 7, 37, 41–77,
151–161, 164, 166, 170
see also Development
expanded, 4, 7
reduced, 4, 7
Resolution, 167
Restructuring, 163–165, 167–168
Revision sequence, 159
Reward, 13
intrinsic, 13, 162
Rhyme, 8–10
Rote, 15–16
Rules, 1–2, 164, 170
superficial, 170

Semantic, 1, 8, 11–13, 159, 163–164, 169
Sibling rivalry, 12
Simultaneous, increase of developmental
patterns, 113, 121, 124, 130, 132,
138
Situation, *see* Environment, Speech
Sleep, 168
Social-context play, 9–11
Social play, 9, 13
Solitary play, 9
Speech, private, 9
see also Crib speech, Monologue, Private speech
Speech setting, 116, 139, 159
mother, 6, 15
social situations of, 166
asocial/self, 38, 42–76
social/other, 38–76
social/self, 38, 41–76
see also Environment
Spontaneous speech, 8–9, 11–12, 14–15,
164
repairs, 12, 17
see also Production
Structure, 18, 159, 164
complex, 17
Substitutions, 3–4, 19, 37, 40–77

see also Development
Suffixes, 167
Syntax, 1, 8, 10–11, 16–17, 25, 169

Transcription of speech samples, 23, 25
Trends, 152
  developmental, 102–103
  group, 43
  see also Development, Relations
Tuning, 163, 164, 167–168
Twins, 10, 13

Utterance, 154–155

combined, 4
complex, 4, 18, 164
model, 3, 18–19, 42, 46, 59, 61, 65,
    68, 73, 77, 153–155, 161, 164–
    165
original, 55
see also Complex utterances

Vocabulary, 170

Within-sample comparison,
    see Development
Word play, 10

```
                99812
 P          Kuczaj, Stan
 118            Crib speech
 .K8            and language
 1983           play
```

DATE DUE